CALIFORNIA'S GOLD RUSH COUNTRY

CALIFORNIA'S GOLD RUSH COUNTRY

A GUIDE TO THE BEST OF THE MOTHER LODE

BARBARA BRAASCH

JOHNSTON
ASSOCIATES
INTERNATIONAL

P. O. BOX 313
MEDINA, WASHINGTON 98039
(206) 454-3490 ▪ FAX: (206) 462-1335
ONLINE ADDRESS: jasibooks@aol.com

California's Gold Rush Country, First Edition
© Copyright 1996 by Barbara Braasch

ISBN 1-881409-14-7

Cover photos courtesy of Larry Angier/Image Photo and Tuolumne County Visitors Bureau. Interior photos courtesy of Martin Litton, Larry Angier, Dick James, Sue Sparks, Golden Chain Council, Knight Foundry, City of Placerville, Sutter Creek Inn, and Tuolumne County Visitors Bureau.

Cover art, book design and production by Mike Jaynes

Disclaimer

Although diligent efforts have been made to confirm the accuracy of information contained in this work, neither the publisher nor the author is responsible for errors or inaccuracies or for changes occurring after publication. This work was not prepared under the sponsorship, license, or authorization of any business, attraction, park, person, or organization described, depicted, or discussed herein.

JASI
Post Office Box 313
Medina, Washington 98039
(206) 454-3490 FAX: (206) 462-1335

Printed in the United States of America

Library of Congress Cataloging-in-Publication Data

Braasch, Barbara.
    California's Gold Rush Country: A Guide to the Best of the
    Mother Lode / Barbara Braasch.
        p.   cm.
    Includes index.
    ISBN 1-881409-14-7
1. California -- Guidebooks. 2. California -- Gold discoveries.
3. Gold mines and mining -- California -- History.   I. Title.
F859.3.B65 1996
917.9404'b3 - dc20   95-49083
                                                               CIP

FOREWORD

Even though the discovery of gold in California occurred nearly a full century and a half ago, the cry of *Eureka!*continues to reverberate around the world. Each year hundreds of thousands of visitors come to California's Gold Rush Country to relive the colorful era of the 49er.

It is a fabled land, a region as rich in history and natural beauty as it is in mineral wealth. California's Gold Rush Country stretches for more than 300 miles along the western slope of the mighty Sierra Nevada. Towering mountains, roaring rivers and lush forests, as well as relics from its colorful past make this area a mecca for tourists.

The region is sometimes referred to as the *Mother Lode* because of a mythical vein of solid gold which was said to run continually north and south for more than 120 miles. The name is attributed to Mexican miners who called it *La Veta Madre*. Myth or not, the region's surface and deep, hardrock mines produced untold millions of dollars and helped finance, among other notable enterprises, the first transcontinental railroad. The discovery of gold also hastened the state's admission to the Union.

California's Gold Rush began and ended with a feverish flurry. Less than two years after the gold-rush-triggering discovery at Sutter's Mill, hundreds of mining camps sprung to life like mushrooms after the first fall rain. During its heyday there were some 550 in the region — 300 have vanished without a trace. Others exist only because they are still spotted on a map, or marked by plaques erected to explain, "Here stood..."

Some of the early camps grew to full-scale communities boasting populations of as many as 5,000. These towns had their own newspapers, fire companies, theaters, banks, brass bands, volunteer militias and even churches — albeit the latter were usually outnumbered 20-to-1 by saloons and gambling halls.

The era of the free wheeling pik-and-pan miner was soon replaced by huge, well-financed concerns that came on the scene to sink deep mine shafts, or wash away entire mountains with powerful streams of water in search of a vein equal to the mother of all veins. Gradually, the rowdy 49ers always on the move for a richer strike, were displaced by a more stable population of hardrock miners imported from Europe and the eastern United States. California's tumultuous Gold Rush lasted by 10 years.

But even today, there are modern prospectors working their claims. You need only drive along Highway 49 to see them. Recreational mining is also popular. In Sierra County, the venerable "Sixteen-to-One Mine" is being reworked. Its owner reports growing profits.

On the eve of the 150th anniversary of that first strike, scores of old California Gold Rush towns survive, not as ghosts marked only by a brass plaque, but as full-fledged communities with commerce actively being carried out in buildings that date from the mid-1800s.

Organizations such as the Golden Chain Council of the Mother Lode have worked to preserve much of the region's revered heritage. The Council also spearheaded a drive for a north-south road that would connect the major town and mines in the region. In 1919, a delegation of council members mounted a lobbying assault upon the state legislature and two years later won approval for State Route 49 — the Golden Chain Highway. It remains the only roadway that links the 11 counties comprising California's Gold Rush Country Region.

"California's Gold Rush Country" vividly portrays the region's past and present. It is a must for first time visitors as well as those more familiar with its historical, cultural and natural attributes.

Wally Lagorio
Director, Golden Chain Council

TABLE OF CONTENTS

SPECIAL FEATURES

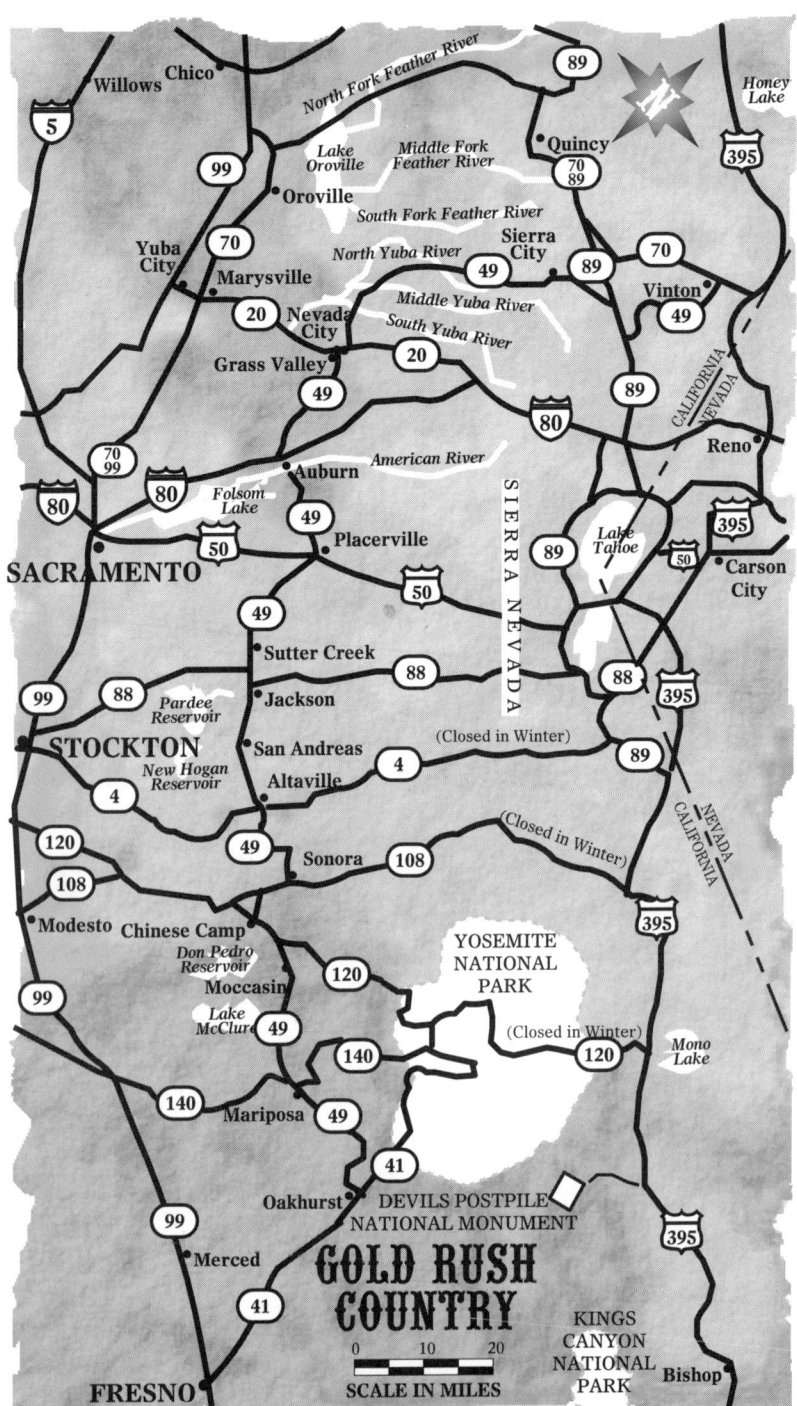

A PEEK INTO THE PAST

"Monday 24th this day some kind of mettle was found in the tail race that looks like goald first discovered by James Martial, the boss of the mill."

With this barely legible diary entry, Henry W. Bigler, a workman at Captain John Sutter's sawmill on the American River in northern California, recorded the moment in January 1848 that would change the course of history.

James Marshall's find focused the attention of the world on California. Within a year his discovery would spawn a great migration that would open the West. A horde of gold-seekers would converge on the territory from all points of the compass, their ardent hunt for the precious metal in every nook and cranny of the Sierra Nevada foothills forming one of the most dramatic chapters in the nation's history.

California's Gold Rush will always be remembered, not only for its historic and economic impact but also for its unique character— and its colorful characters: John C. Fremont, Joaquin Murieta, Bret Harte, Black Bart, Lola Montez, and many more. Extremes were the order of the day, and there are literally hundreds of stories about this era that cause listeners to shake their heads in wonder and disbelief. Though some anecdotes are tall tales, others are not exaggerated. Towns really did grow up overnight and disappear almost as fast.

Today less than half of the 500 mining camps spawned between 1848 and 1860 still stand. Most were flimsy and temporary to begin with, and 140 years of harsh weather, human neglect, and the inexorable march of progress took their toll. Some disappeared entirely; others are little more than crumbling foundations and names on signposts.

A few, such as Sonora, Jackson, Placerville, Auburn, and Grass Valley, have become prosperous towns with landmark brick and stone buildings testifying to proud Gold Rush origins. State historic parks preserve the former boomtowns of Columbia and North Bloomfield. Sutter's reconstructed sawmill is the centerpiece of Coloma State Historic Park.

The Argonauts

Fortune-hunting prospectors were called "Forty-niners" in reference to the first big year of the Gold Rush, but some arrived as early as 1848 and others as late as 1853. In the spring of 1848 there were less than 15,000 people in California, not counting Native Americans. A state census in 1852 revealed that the non-Native population had swelled to almost 225,000.

Historians estimate that 65 to 75 percent of the miners busy digging for gold in the California foothills came from other parts of the nation. Some 100,000 arrived from the East via overland routes, and the rest either braved a voyage around the Horn or endured two voyages and a miserable trek across the Isthmus of Panama.

An estimated 5,000 Chileans arrived in California during the first six months of 1849, and the number of Mexican "commuters" was even higher. (Mexicans worked in the mines during the dry season and returned to their homes when the winter rains arrived.)

Potato famine, economic depression, and social upheavals in the British Isles prompted a number of English, Scots, Irish, and Welsh to seek their fortunes. Many of them brought valuable mining experience to the gold fields. Political instability and crop losses also encouraged a large emigration from Germany and France.

Though the Chinese got a late start, they quickly made up for lost time. In 1850, there were only 600 Chinese in California. By 1852, their numbers had grown to 25,000.

Life in the Camps

Most adventurers arrived in response to stories of big strikes: nuggets as big as your fists lying on the ground just waiting to be picked up by passersby. The naive thought the gravels would be rich enough to yield a lifetime fortune in a single panful. The truth was that mining was miserable drudgery, filled with disappointments. Miners often worked long hours in icy streams or deep inside the tunnels of quartz mines to dig out just enough gold to pay the astronomical prices of bed and board.

Some lucky finds were made: miners near Carson Hill once dug up a single gold nugget weighing 195 pounds and a 141-pound nugget was unearthed near Sierra City. However, an early miner might have to pay a dollar for a slice of bread and another dollar to butter it, $50 for the shovel with which to dig his fortune, and $100 for a blanket or a horse. The ones who really struck it rich were those who supplied the miners with food, clothing, tools, transportation, and amusement.

A miner's life was simple. When not grubbing for gold, his recreation usually consisted of playing cards or exchanging the latest rumors of strikes. Occasionally a traveling circus, theatrical

GOING TO SEE THE ELEPHANT

The phrase, "going to see the elephant," came to mean the excitement the argonauts felt at the possibility of finding gold. The phrase supposedly originated from a story about a farmer who had heard of elephants but had never seen one. When a circus came to a nearby town, he loaded his wagon and started out, determined to see this creature.

On the way, he met the circus parade, led by the elephant. The farmer was delighted but his horses were terrified. They bucked, overturned his wagon, spilling the cargo, and ran away. "I don't give a hang," said the farmer. "I have seen the elephant."

troupe, or bull and bear fight broke up the monotony. Only the largest settlements had saloons and fandango halls, and women were few and far between. At most dances you could only tell the "ladies" from the gentlemen by noting which had the handkerchief tied around his arm.

When California attained statehood in 1850, gold camps were crowded with men (and some women) who had come to make their fortunes. By 1873, however, only 30,000 miners remained in the gold fields, and more than half of them were persistent Chinese who laboriously reworked the gravels that presumably weren't worth anyone else's efforts.

Some prospectors went home disillusioned by the hard realities of mining; others left because of persecution by hard-nosed Yankees who ran "furriners" out of the best diggings. Though few got rich from the Gold Rush, many found a new way of life in California and stayed around to make notable contributions to the state's rapid economic growth. Some went to work for the big commercial quartz and hydraulic mining operations that thrived for another 30 years or more. Others found employment in peripheral industries that supplied the mines—mills, iron foundries, and machine shops. Those who had temporarily adopted mining because of its get-rich-quick aspects returned to their old professions.

The rush for gold was over by 1884. A few of the largest mines continued operations, but fixed gold prices, high production costs, and World War II brought about their demise in 1942.

MINERS' TEN COMMANDMENTS

In the early days of free-for-all mining, prospectors were forced to write their own laws. These wry regulations gradually spread throughout the camps, becoming known as the Miners' Ten Commandments. They were enacted into Federal law in 1853.

Here is a condensed version:

1. Thou shalt have no other claim than one.

2. Thou shalt not make any false claim or jump one. If thou do thou must go prospecting and shall hire thy body out to make thy board and save thy bacon.

3. Thou shalt not go prospecting before thy claim gives out. Neither shall thee take thy gold to the gambling table in vain.

4. Thou shalt remember the Sabbath. Six days thou mayest dig, for in six days labor thou canst work enough to wear out thy body in two years.

5. Thou shalt not think more of thy gold than how thou shall enjoy it.

6. Thou shalt not kill thy body by working in the rain. Neither shall thou destroy thyself by getting "tight" nor "high seas over" while drinking down thy purse.

7. Thou shalt not grow discouraged, nor think of going home before thou hast made thy pile.

8. Thou shalt not steal a pick, a shovel or a pan from thy fellow miners, nor borrow a claim, nor pan out gold from others riffle box. They will hang thee, or brand thee like a horse thief with the letter R upon thy cheek.

9. Thou shalt not tell any false tales about "good diggings" in the mountains, lest your neighbors return with naught but a rifle and present thee with its contents thereof and thou shall fall down and die.

10. Thou shall not commit unsuitable matrimony nor neglect thy first love. If thy heart be free thou shall "pop the question" like a man, lest another more manly than thou art should step in before thee, and then your lot be that of a poor, despised confortless bachelor.

How Gold Was Mined in the Mother Lode

Finding gold in the California foothills depended on a great deal of luck; getting the gold out of the ground depended on hard, back-breaking work. It is true that some of the miners were able to pick up free gold, chisel nuggets out of crevices with a pocket knife, and get thousands of dollars worth of dust in a single pan. But those rich rewards belonged only to a few who were lucky enough to be the first to make a strike at some very rich diggings. Most argonauts who eagerly traveled to the gold fields expecting to pick up nuggets off the ground, turned away disillusioned when they realized the amount of hard labor required to get a day's wages.

Gold mined in the Sierra Nevada foothills came from lode and placer deposits. Lode (hardrock) deposits contain native gold, mostly in quartz veins, that ascended in mineralized solutions from deep within the earth. Placer deposits contain gold originally in lode deposits which, through erosion, have been moved to other locations. Water has always been the principal moving force in forming placer deposits.

Panning for gold

Panning was the simplest way to separate placer gold from dirt and rocks. The basic procedure was to shovel gold-bearing gravels into a shallow pan, add some water, and then carefully swirl the mixture around so the water and light material spilled over the side and the heavy stuff, including gold, settled to the bottom of the pan. The trouble with this method is the time involved. About 20 minutes was needed to wash a single pan and pick up the fine particles of gold. On a good day, one miner could only wash about 50 pans.

Rocking the cradle

A rocker was simply a rectangular wooden box set on a slope and mounted on rockers. The top had a sieve and the bottom consisted of a series of cleats or riffles. Dirt was poured into the top, followed by a bucket of water. The cradle was then rocked to agitate the mixture and send it flowing through the box. Big rocks were caught in the sieve, the waste ran out the lower end with the water, and the heavy gold fell to the bottom of the box and was caught on the cleats.

The rocker had many advantages. It could be made quickly and moved from site to site. Since water was added by the bucketful, no continuous source was needed, and the rocker became popular at dry diggings where water had to be carried by hand. But the main advantage was that one miner could wash a lot more dirt with a cradle than he could with a pan, and two men working together could wash a cubic yard a day.

Though the rocker and the gold pan worked reasonably well for coarse gold, they were inefficient at trapping the fine particles of "flour" gold. To increase their take from each load, miners began adding small amounts of mercury to the bottom of the cradle. Mercury has the unique propensity to trap fine gold while passing by almost everything else. Periodically, the miners would remove the mercury and heat it. As it vaporized, only the free gold was left in the retort.

Using a Long Tom

The Long Tom was an enlarged and modified cradle. It consisted of a 10- to 20-foot trough, about a foot wide, fitted with a sheet of perforated metal. The riffle box was located underneath the metal sheet. At least two men shoveled the pay dirt into the top of the Long Tom. A third man in the crew threw out big rocks as they collected and kept the dirt moving through the box. Once or twice a day, the gold and sand caught on the riffles would be removed and panned.

The Long Tom could handle a lot of dirt, but it needed a continuous source of fast-moving water. This meant that the miners either had to locate on the bank of a river or dig ditches to bring the water to the site of the rich dry dirt.

Sluicing

Sluice boxes were longer versions of the Long Tom, built on the theory that more gold would precipitate if the length of the riffle boxes were extended. A number of sluice boxes were often fastened together in a long line, and a whole crew of miners was kept busy shoveling dirt and gravel into the troughs.

Ground sluicing was practiced in a number of ways. One method was to dig a shallow ditch and divert enough river water to soften the soil. Then the miners would toss the loosened material into a sluice box at the bottom of the ditch. The gold was removed from the box by panning.

Quartz mining

It was with hardrock operations that gold mining in California became a business rather than an adventure. The first quartz mine in California was opened in 1849 at Mariposa, but this system of mining hit its peak in the Northern Mines, particularly around Grass Valley.

Digging the gold-bearing quartz out of the ground was done in two ways. Tunnels were used when the hillside was steep enough to allow a horizontal entrance to be dug into the mountain. Ore was then loaded into mine cars and taken directly to the mill. The other method required sinking either a vertical or incline shaft and digging "drifts" to intersect the vein at various levels. The incline shaft followed the vein as it descended into the earth, usually between the angles of 30 to 50 degrees.

Once the ore was brought above ground, it had to be crushed. The first crushing equipment was the Mexican arrastra, which pulverized rocks between a stationary stone slab and a moving stone slab. The best crusher was the vertical stamp mill. The hammers of these big stamps were lifted by steam and dropped by gravity in a noisy rotation that pounded the ore into workable dust.

Separating the gold from the pulverized ore by panning proved very inefficient. A process was developed that passed gold-bearing materials over amalgamation plates to trap the fine gold with mercury. The amalgamation was retorted to capture the gold, and the gold was melted and cast into bars. To increase gold recovery to over 90 percent, tailings from the amalgamation process were then treated by adding cyanide.

Dredging

Wherever there was enough water to build them, big dredgers could be used to work deep gold-bearing gravels. Buckets could dig up material as much as 100 feet below the water level and dump it into a floating processing plant. The gravels were screened, jiggled, and washed to separate rock from gold and sand. The heavy material was finally forced into barrels where copper plates covered with mercury trapped the gold. The waste was pumped out the rear of the dredger into huge piles that forever changed the landscape. Dredging was first tried in the 1850s, but it did not become popular or profitable until the early 1900s.

Hydraulic mining

This type of mining was the most efficient method of getting gold out of the ground, but it was also the most destructive to the countryside. The operating principle was very simple: if water under pressure could be directed against a bank of soft gravels, the gravels would disintegrate very rapidly and the dirt would wash downhill into a series of huge sluice boxes that would catch the gold.

Hydraulicking was introduced in California in 1853 by E. E. Matteson, a Nevada City miner. His was a very simple operation, with a small volume of water carried through a canvas hose and spewed out through a primitive nozzle fabricated out of sheet metal. Enterprising miners quickly saw the possibilities of hydraulicking, and procedures became more sophisticated. Iron pipe and good hoses replaced the canvas, and big nozzles were fabricated under the names of Monitor and Giant.

The key to the operation was a constant source of water. Some of the big nozzles were nine inches in diameter and required 30,000 gallons of water a minute. To get the water to the mining sites, very expensive systems of flumes and ditches had to be dug. It is estimated that by 1859, some 5,000 miles of canals and viaducts stretched across the countryside, the majority in the Northern Mines. Single lines were as much as 15 to 20 miles long.

The water line always came into a mining area at a high elevation so that a natural drop of 100 to 400 feet would generate enough force to build up high pressure at the nozzle.

The power of a hydraulic nozzle is hard to describe. One historian compares it with turning a modern fire hose on a sand pile or a bank of snow. Whole mountain slopes could be devoured in a day, with the gravels rushing down through the sluices and out into piles of waste. It was this waste or "slickins" that led to the downfall of hydraulic mining. It clogged the rivers, caused floods in farmlands, disrupted agriculture, and even discolored San Francisco Bay. Finally, miners were ordered to quit hydraulicking unless they could dispose of the waste; this was impossible so the method was abandoned.

Despite the high volumes of gravels that could be mined by hydraulicking, the system was not very efficient and a lot of gold got away in the fast-moving water that poured through the sluices. The tailings were rich enough to warrant another mining, and enterprising miners working behind the hydraulickers often did very well.

Unique Architecture

The divergent backgrounds of the people who flocked to California's gold-rich fields from 1849 to 1870 are reflected in the architectural styles of the buildings you see throughout the Gold Country. Structures like the Methodist church in Sutter Creek, with its cornice and classic low-pitched gable, appear to have been moved directly from New England village greens.

Photo courtesy of Larry Angier

I.O.O.F. Hall, Jackson, Amador County

The influence of the old South is most often seen in the Central Mother Lode. The hot, sunny climate resembled that south of the Mason-Dixon line, so buildings were designed with single, double, or multistoried porches—sometimes on all four sides. Usually narrow, the porches served as sun screens rather than living spaces. Iron railings, such as those used on the Prince and Garibardi store in Altaville, the Yuba Canal building in Nevada City, the old Masonic Hall in Auburn, and the Murphys Hotel, can also be attributed to Southern influence.

Early-day building was done with readily available materials, usually local country stone and wood from nearby forests. Few structures were built of adobe because of unsuitable weather and soil. The rammed-earth building in Fiddletown and the replica created in Coloma are the best examples of this type of architecture. Brick was generally regarded as a status symbol, and most brick-front structures have fieldstone sides.

Architecture also differed by region. Some elements may exist only in one county, or in widely separate areas. Buildings in Calaveras County, for example, tend to have asymmetrical or square high hip roofs. Auburn's brick buildings often feature the jack arch and partial attic story.

Although the Gold Country was a frontier region and time was of the essence, a great deal of craftsmanship went into a building. Towns struggled against tremendous odds to maintain a continuous style of architecture, even during the days when fire often destroyed whole settlements overnight. Supposedly, a disastrous fire in Grass Valley inspired the iron shutters and heavy masonry walls that now stand throughout the region. Certainly tin roofs were used as a fire deterrent.

After 1870, commercial hardrock mining took over, other businesses proliferated, new people came to town, and architecture took on the contemporary Victorian style so well portrayed by Nevada City residences.

USING THIS GUIDE

This book covers the region along the western slopes of the Sierra Nevada between Madera County to the south and Sierra County to the north. The area ranges in altitude from rolling grassland several hundred feet above sea level to the 6,700-foot elevation of fir-clad, often snowy Yuba Pass. Though by no means all of California's gold-bearing land, this was the major gold belt and the scene of most of the action during Gold Rush days.

Getting There

Appropriately numbered State Highway 49 winds through the Gold Country, providing access to most large towns. The road stays at around 2,000 feet, except where it dips into deep river canyons or climbs up the high mountain pass above Downieville. You can probably drive its 310 twisting miles in a day or two, but you won't see much. For a pretty thorough reconnaissance of the whole area, you need about four days, to allow time for side trips to some of the most meaningful places. Perhaps the best way to see the Gold Country is simply to explore it section by section a few days at a time.

Most of the roads mentioned are paved, although only a few stretches of Highway 49 could be regarded as freeway. Some of the side trips involve driving over dirt roads, all passable during the summer. In the higher elevations of the northern Sierra, snow will often keep back roads closed well into the summer.

In remote areas, be sure to have plenty of gasoline and be prepared for an impromptu picnic. Gas stations, grocery stores, restaurants, and overnight accommodations may be few and far between if you venture far off main highways. Yet it's these same back roads that lead to places little changed since they were glimpsed by the first argonauts.

Keep a sharp eye out for crumbling walls, scarred hillsides, tailings, rusted mining equipment, and overgrown cemeteries. Often these are the only remnants of a once boisterous, prosperous settlement. Tombstones often tell terse tales of a prospector's unfilled dreams.

Where to Go

The three main chapters in this book are based on an arbitrary division of the Gold Rush Country—Southern Mines, Central Mother Lode, and Northern Mines. Each area is distinctly different in appearance and allure: the Southern Mines region is still delightfully rural; the more heavily populated Central Mother Lode is best known for its wealth of photogenic towns and colorful annual events; and the spectacular scenery of the Northern Mines is as big a draw as its Gold Rush mementos.

Each chapter contains a general introduction to the area and a map showing the route covered in the text. Interesting stops along Highway 49 and detours off the main road are highlighted. Information on the largest towns includes selective suggestions for lodging, dining, recreation, and off-road detours. Rather than list all of the available options in each community, this guide mentions only a few "nuggets," which are either personal picks or the best of what's available. For complete accommodation, dining, and recreation choices, contact local chambers of commerce at the addresses listed at the back of this chapter. AAA members will find listings in the California TourBook.

Hotels, motels, inns, and restaurants are usually open daily from Memorial Day to Labor Day and on weekends the rest of the year. Unless otherwise noted, lodging prices at well-established inns range from inexpensive to fairly expensive ($65 to $150). With few exceptions, restaurant meals are bargains.

Accommodations:
$$$ expensive (most rooms $150 and up)
$$ moderate (most rooms $65 to $149)
$ inexpensive (most rooms under $64)

Restaurants:
$$$ expensive (most meals over $20)
$$ moderate (most meals $15 to $19
$ inexpensive (most meals under $14)

When to Visit

Every season has its advantages. Gold panning is best in the spring when streams are filled by snow melt in the higher mountains. If you're planning on swimming in some of the deep rivers, better wait until the summer sun has a chance to warm icy depths.

At the lower elevations, spring usually arrives early in February and March. La Porte may still have snow in April or May, but the lower foothills are carpeted in green grass by that time. As days grow longer, blazing Scotch broom brightens mile after mile of hillsides, and lupine, owl's clover, Mariposa lily, buttercup, brodiaea, Mexican firebush, and California poppy enliven meadows.

Summer brings the most tourists to the Gold Country. The weather is likely to be fiercely hot at low elevations and pleasant in the higher pine belt. You'll need reservations for overnight accommodations as this is the time when theatrical groups perform and most colorful events take place. Shops, museums, and historical attractions are more likely to be open daily at this time.

The Gold Country seems best named in the fall as changing leaves provide a bright contrast to the rolling golden hills. Autumn's rains settle summer dust and wash oaks, poplars, locusts, and maples just in time for them to brighten old towns with splashes of yellow and vermilion.

Winter is the snow season and many ski resorts (Kirkwood, Bear Valley, Dodge Ridge) operate a few miles east of Highway 49. It's a good time for Christmas shopping in gaily decorated stores and lingering in front of a fireplace in a cozy inn. Many old ruins look better under a dusting of snow than they do in the heat of August.

Additional Resources

For a detailed map on Gold Country attractions along Highway 49, send $3 to the Golden Chain Council of the Mother Lode (P.O. Box 5142, Marysville, CA 95901; phone 916/755-4949), an organization of 11 member counties. Maps, brochures, and walking tours are also dispensed generously and enthusiastically by visitor associations in the following areas:

SOUTHERN MINES

Coulterville Chamber of Commerce
5007 Main Street
P.O. Box 333
Coulterville, CA 95311
(209) 878-3074

Eastern Madera County Chamber of Commerce
49074 Civic Circle
P.O. Box 1414
Oakhurst, CA 93644
(209) 683-4636

Mariposa County Chamber of Commerce
5158 Highway 140
P.O. Box 425
Mariposa, CA 95338
(209) 966-2456

Tuolumne County Visitors Bureau
55 W. Stockton Road
P.O. Box 4020
Sonora, CA 95370
(209) 533-4420
(800) 446-1333

CENTRAL MOTHER LODE

Amador County Chamber of Commerce
P.O. Box 596
125 Peek Street
Jackson, CA 95642
(209) 223-0350

Calaveras County Lodging & Visitor Association
P. O. Box 637
1301 Main Street
Angels Camp, CA 95222
(209) 736-0049
(800) 225-3764

El Dorado County Chamber of Commerce
542 Main Street
Placerville, CA 95667
(916) 621-5885
(800) 457-6279

Placer County Tourism Authority
13460-A Lincoln Way
Auburn, CA 95603
(916) 887-2111

NORTHERN MINES

Grass Valley/Nevada County Chamber of Commerce
248 Mill Street
Grass Valley, CA 95945
(916) 273-4667

Nevada City Chamber of Commerce
132 Main Street
Nevada City, CA 95959
(916) 265-2692

Sierra County Chamber of Commerce
P.O. Box 206
Loyalton, CA 96118
(916) 993-6900
(800) 200-4949

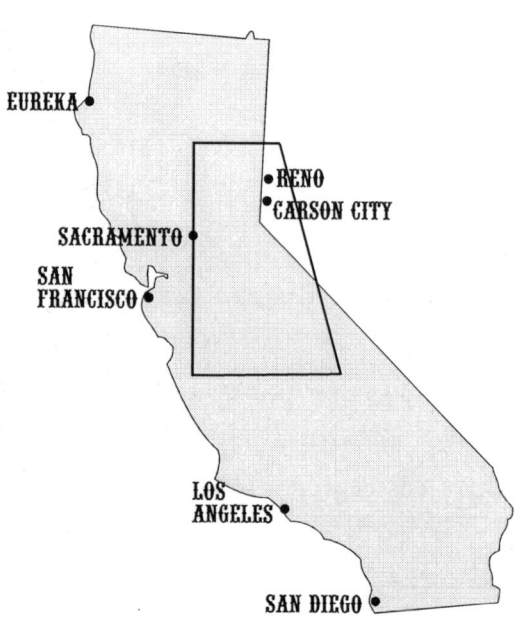

Knight Foundry in Sutter Creek, Amador County

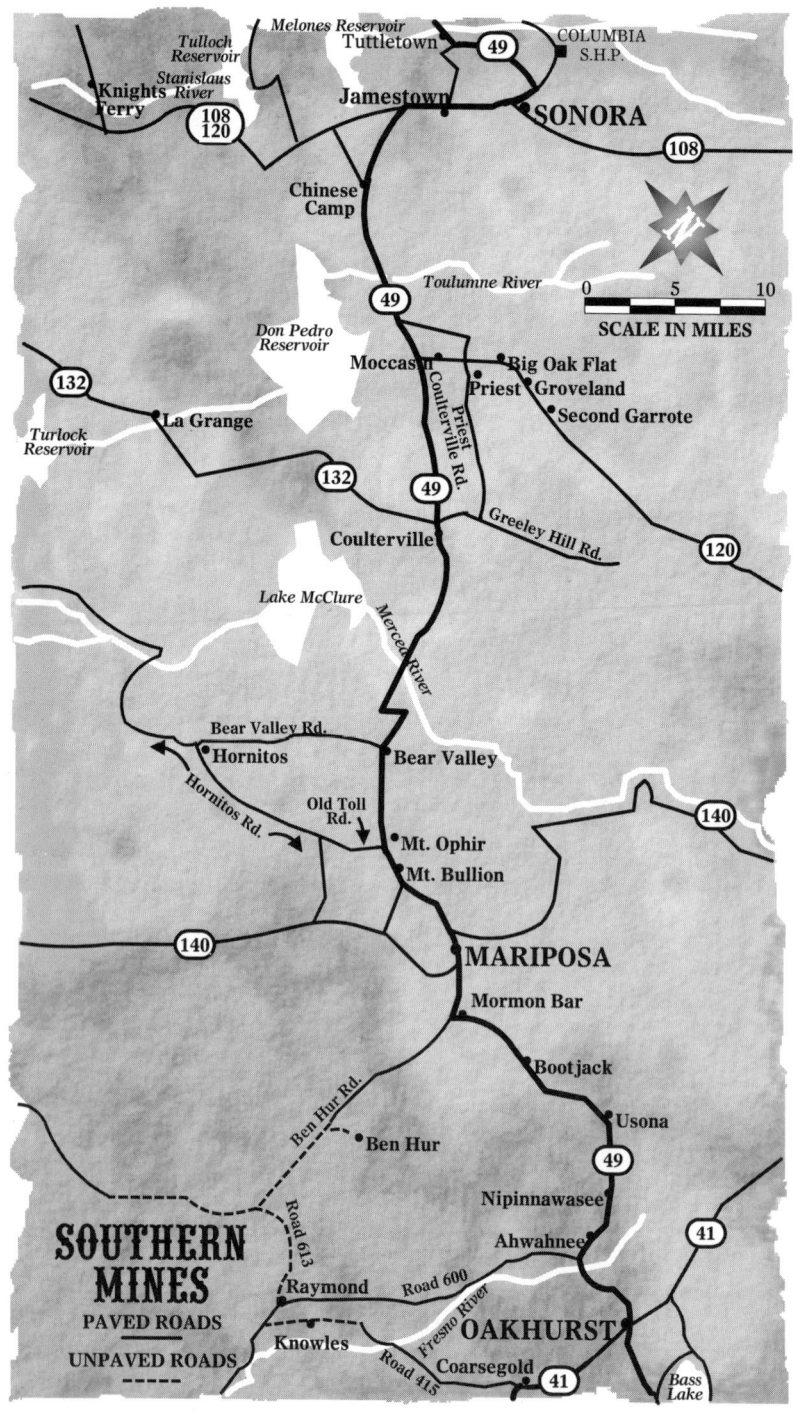

Melones Reservoir
Tulloch Reservoir
Tuttletown
49
COLUMBIA S.H.P.
Knights Ferry
Stanislaus River
Jamestown
108
120
SONORA
108

Chinese Camp

Toulumne River
49
0   5   10
SCALE IN MILES

Don Pedro Reservoir
Moccasin
Big Oak Flat
132
Priest
Groveland
La Grange
Priest Coulterville Rd.
Second Garrote

Turlock Reservoir
132
49
Greeley Hill Rd.
120

Coulterville

Lake McClure
Mercer River

Bear Valley Rd.
Hornitos
Bear Valley
Hornitos Rd.
Old Toll Rd.
140
Mt. Ophir
Mt. Bullion

140
MARIPOSA

Mormon Bar

Bootjack

Ben Hur Rd.
Usona
Ben Hur
49

SOUTHERN MINES
Nipinnawasee
Road 613
Ahwahnee
41
Raymond
Road 600
Fresno River
PAVED ROADS
OAKHURST
UNPAVED ROADS
Knowles
Road 415
Coarsegold
41
Bass Lake

SOUTHERN MINES

old had been discovered in small quantities along rivers as far south as Madera County before the announcement of James Marshall's find farther north in 1848; however, it took a while for miners to leave the well-publicized areas and trickle down to the Southern Mines.

Though the placer and quartz veins in this part of the country never rivaled those to the north, the region was well known to Mexican ranchers and Indian traders. The eventual discovery of Yosemite Valley by white men brought tourists almost as soon as it did prospectors.

The area is still sparsely settled. In fact, the section between Oakhurst and Mariposa is virtually overlooked in most books dealing with California's gold discovery. But Oakhurst is the southern terminus of Highway 49, the Mother Lode Highway, and some of the surrounding mines were as famous as any in the Gold Country.

Oakhurst

Named Fresno Flats when it was originally settled in the mid-1850s a short way from the present site, Oakhurst was never a typical mining town because there was little gold in the immediate vicinity. The nearest major mine was the Enterprise, about five miles downstream on the Fresno River.

Today's visitors must dig to find traces of this bustling little community's history. Most of the once-booming mining camps around the area have passed into oblivion, and the few small communities that survive appear to have turned their backs on their turbulent past. Some like String Town and Poison Switch are just colorful names.

One survivor is the little New England-style Christ Church, built in 1891 in Fresno Flats. Renamed the Little Church on the Hill and moved to its present location in 1957, the structure crowns a knoll in the old Oakhurst cemetery on Highway 41. Surrounding tombstones tell a little of the area's history. One monument marks the final resting place of a Lieutenant Skeens, who was one of the Army officers killed in 1851 during the Mariposa Indian War near Ahwahnee.

Historic Attractions

Fresno Flats Historical Park

49777 Road 427 off Highway 41
Oakhurst
209/683-6570

Tours of this outdoor museum give much of the flavor of early-day family life. Weathered treasures include a log cabin dating back to 1867, a two-story farmhouse, an old schoolhouse, a courthouse containing the Nathan Sweet Museum, the 19th-century Fresno Flats jail, a jail from nearby Raymond, a blacksmith shop, and a variety of antique wagons. *Open Wednesday through Saturday 1 to 3 P.M., until 4 P.M. Sunday. Admission $2 adults, 75 cents children 5 through 12. Picnic area.*

Sierra Mono Indian Museum

Intersection of Roads 225 and 228
North Fork
209/877-2115

An eclectic collection of Native American artifacts (baskets, bead-work tools, arrowheads, and more) plus a wildlife display is housed in a stone-front structure. An annual Indian Fair on the first weekend in August features dancing, crafts, and food. *Open weekends. Adults $2, children $1.*

Wassama Round House State Historic Park

Off Highway 49 on
Round House Road, Ahwahnee
209/683-8869

This ceremonial round house was built in 1975 by local Miwoks to replace an original structure that dated from the 1860s. Native American dances and demonstrations take place in mid-July. *Open weekends. Admission $1. Picnic area.*

Photo courtesy of Martin Litton

Fresno Flats Historic Park, Oakhurst

SAVAGE—
SOLDIER, MINER, TRADER

Though James Savage spent considerable time in the southern part of the Gold Country, his first destination in California was Sutter's Fort, where he arrived in 1846 with an emigrant party from Illinois. The hardships of that trip claimed the lives of his wife and child.

After a few months as a soldier in John C. Fremont's California Battalion, he went to work for John Sutter at his fort, and Sutter's diary records that Savage worked with James Marshall on the construction of the now-famous mill.

In 1848, he drifted southward and began mining at Woods Diggings and Jamestown. Discovering that a fortune could be made by supplying goods in exchange for gold, Savage made friends with the Miwok tribe and learned many of their dialects.

In the spring of 1850, Savage was warned that the Native Americans had decided to drive the invaders from their land. Raids were made on his trading posts on Mariposa Creek and on the Fresno River (four miles from the present site of Coarsegold), and several of his employees were murdered.

Though many thought this was Savage's private war, 74 volunteer miner-fighters responded to a call for help, and the Mariposa Battalion was formed. On patrol on March 25, 1851, Savage and his men entered Yosemite Valley, becoming its first white explorers. They also captured Chief Tenaya.

After the uprising was quelled, Savage resumed trading and regained the allegiance of the Indians through a combination of awe and fear. He used little magic tricks like burning oil on a pan of water and claiming he had the power to burn up all the rivers. He also used a battery to deliver shocks, declaring he had the powers of great gods.

Savage's popularity and prosperity aroused much jealousy among the locals. Major Walter H. Harvey, a rival trader, spearheaded an attack which caused the deaths of several of the Native Americans working for Savage. Claiming Harvey was responsible, Savage took Harvey up on a boast that he was afraid to meet on Harvey's own territory. During a fist fight, Savage's pistol fell from his shirt and Harvey killed him.

Some questions remain unanswered, especially the issue of what happened to the fortune Savage supposedly acquired in his prosperous trading posts. When his grave was opened all that was found, in addition to fragments of bone, was a piece of Chinese pottery, a rusted squirrel trap, broken bits of glass bottles, and a piece of metal framework for an old-fashioned purse.

Recreation

Yosemite Mountain Sugar Pine Railroad

15 miles northeast of Oakhurst
via Highway 41, Fish Camp
209/683-7273

Steam train rides (call for times): adults $10, children 3 through 12 $5 (less for Jenny gas-powered engine). Railroad museum and gift shop. Take a four-mile steam- or gas-powered narrow gauge railroad excursion over tracks built in 1899 by the Madera Sugar Pine Lumber Company. *Open daily mid-April to mid-October.*

Bass Lake

About 18 miles south of Oakhurst
209/642-3676

Facilities at this popular man-made lake include three marinas, lodges, restaurants, and a theater. *Open for summer camping, hiking, boating, fishing, and water skiing.*

Lodging

Chateau du Sureau

48688 Victoria Lane,
Oakhurst, CA 93644
209/683-6860 $$$

For a special splurge, reserve a room in the French-style country house Erma Kubin-Clanin built for her Elderberry House diners (see below). All nine rooms have canopied beds, antiques, fireplaces, and tiled baths. Rates include breakfast.

Yosemite Gateway Inn

40530 Highway 41
Oakhurst, CA 93644
209/583-2378 $$

A three-night minimum stay in high season is the only drawback to this nicely landscaped, 118-room motel. Among the amenities are swimming pools, spas, and a small fitness center.

Ducey's on the Lake

Bass Lake
CA 93604
209/642-3131   **$$-$$$**

This luxury resort replaced an older, more spartan lakeside lodge. The 20 well-appointed rooms have fireplaces, wet bars and decks. There's a two-night minimum stay in season.

Mariott's Tenaya Lodge

1122 Highway 41
Fish Camp, CA 93623
209/683-6555   **$$$**

A convenient location for the Yosemite-bound, an acclaimed dining room, and nicely landscaped grounds make this attractive 200-room lodge very popular. You'll need reservations well in advance.

Narrow Gauge Inn

48571 Highway 41
Fish Camp, CA 93623
209/683-7720   **$$**

Reserve early for this nicely situated, 27-room inn with a dining room. It's just four miles south of Yosemite. Private balconies or decks let you enjoy the fine forest view.

Dining

Erna's Elderberry House

Highway 41 and Victoria Lane
Oakhurst
209/683-6800   **$$$**

This elegant restaurant has an international reputation for fine continental cuisine and its attractive presentation. Six-course *prix fixe* dinners. *Open for lunch Wednesday through Friday, brunch Sunday, and dinner daily except Tuesday; reservations almost a must.*

Side Trip

Coarsegold to Raymond

A 50-mile back-road loop leads through rolling countryside west of Oakhurst, past hamlets rich in history. The century-old stone fences were built by early Chinese laborers, each of whom was paid 25 cents a day to lay 25 feet of stone.

Coarsegold, a picturesquely named former mining town eight miles south of Oakhurst on Highway 41, acquired instant fame when the first prospectors began picking up gold nuggets from creek beds. A single nugget worth $15,000 was the beginning of a claim called Texas Flats, one of the oldest, deepest, and most extensively worked hard-rock mines in the Southern Mines.

Granite from quarries around Knowles was used to rebuild San Francisco after the 1906 earthquake. To reach the tiny community from Coarsegold, follow Road 415 to Road 606 and jog south. Note the old granite church and a score of foundations that serve as perpetual monuments to wooden structures long since victims of decay, fire, and vandalism.

Raymond was originally named Wildcat Station, not for its lifestyle, but for the tasty stew served to stagecoach travelers on their way to Yosemite. Today, the town is a quiet agricultural community with a minor quarry. To get there from Knowles, take Road 606 about a mile south to Road 600 and turn north.

Road 600 joins Highway 49 just south of the apple-growing area of Ahwahnee. About 5 miles west of this junction, an overgrown cemetery and gaping holes in the hillside are all that mark the site of Grub Gulch, once the largest mountain mining community in the Southern Mines. It is said that whiskey was used to fight fires because it was more available than water. Although Grub Gulch never had a church, five saloons were active day and night.

Mariposa & North

The pretty little town of Mariposa (Spanish for "butterfly") has served as the county seat since 1850. It was once part of the 45,000-acre tract bought for $3,200 by famed explorer and army officer General John C. Fremont. The town's weekly newspaper has been published continuously since 1854.

The Mariposa Mine, near the south end of town, was discovered by Kit Carson and Alex Goody in 1849. Production continued into the 20th century, hitting its peak between 1900 and 1915. (You can see the mine entrance from the back of St. Joseph's Catholic Church on Bullion Street.)

Gold Rush-era survivors on the main street include the Trabucco warehouse and store, the I.O.O.F. Hall, and the balconied Schlageter Hotel Building. One block to the east on Jones Street stands a forbidding stone jail (once the Mother Lode's largest) built in 1859. Some of the tombstones in the cemetery at the northwest edge of town date back over a century.

Mariposa's choicest architectural structure sits atop a quiet hill on Bullion Street. The two-story wooden courthouse (oldest in the state) has been remodeled only slightly since it opened in 1854. The second-floor courtroom contains many original furnishings, and the original tower clock has tolled out the hours since 1866. Free guided tours of the courthouse (open weekdays year-round) are offered weekends from April to October.

Six miles north of Mariposa lies Mount Bullion. Little remains to suggest the feverish activity of the 2,000 men who worked the placers in 1850 and then turned to the rich quartz veins. The Princeton Mine, south of town, produced more than four million dollars in gold. Another Trabucco store and the Princeton Saloon still stand.

From the few buildings still standing in Bear Valley, it's hard to imagine that 3,000 people lived here at the height of the Gold Rush. Nothing remains of the ranch house from where John Fremont ruled his extensive empire, but his story is told in the museum inside the I.O.O.F. Hall. Another interesting relic of the past is the Trabucco store.

FREMONT–
A WESTERN PIONEER

Born in 1813, John C. Fremont was one of those who didn't strike it rich as a miner in California's gold fields. By the time of the discovery, he had married the daughter of popular U.S. Senator Thomas Hart Benton, produced some excellent topographic maps of Missouri River territory, traveled the Rockies with Kit Carson, and led the first winter crossing of the Sierra.

In 1847, Fremont gave his agent, Thomas Larkin, $3,000 and instructions to buy an attractive piece of land near Mission San Jose where he could retire in peace from a tumultuous army career. But for some reason, Larkin instead bought 45,000 acres of dry land in the Sierra foothills.

Fremont was livid until he found that gold had been discovered on his property. When he realized the extent of the gold, the former soldier extended the boundaries of his original purchase up into the hills to take in even more land, most of which had already been claimed by others. He ended up with a single piece of property extending from the Merced River south to Bridgeport.

With this wealth behind him, Fremont moved into the political forefront and became one of California's leading citizens. He was the first (but unsuccessful) U. S. presidential candidate of the fledging Republican Party in 1856.

Upon returning to his Mariposa land in 1857, Fremont discovered that absentee ownership, bad management, and costly lawsuits filed by miners who had been uprooted by his land grab were eating up all of the tremendous profits from the mine. Even though he built a home at Bear Valley for his family and began to personally supervise his huge empire, overhead costs, personal expenses, and legal involvements resulted in no profits.

Things went from bad to worse. Fremont's very controversial military campaigning during the Civil War and his political opposition to Abraham Lincoln cost him his military commands, his political influence, and finally his public prestige. In 1863, the Mariposa property had to be sold for a fraction of its worth. Fremont received enough from the sale to live comfortably, but he managed to lose it all through unwise railroad speculations during the next decade. He died penniless in 1890 in New York, but he is scarcely forgotten in the West. His name has been given to more streets, towns, peaks, and landmarks than any other Western pioneer.

Historic Attractions

Mariposa County History Center
12th and Jessie streets
Mariposa
209/966-2924

For the best overview of Mariposa history, from Native American to mining days, visit this lively museum and library. Among extensive Gold Rush memorabilia is a re-creation of the interior of the Gagliardo Store, which once stood in nearby Hornitos. Outside are an operating five-stamp mill and a Native village. *Open daily April through October; weekends only the rest of the year (closed January). Donations requested.*

Photo courtesy of the Golden Chain Council

Stamp Mill, Mariposa's California State Mining and Mineral Museum

California State Mining and Mineral Museum

Mariposa County Fairgrounds
south of town
209/742-7625

Inside this replica of an 1890s mining complex is a "don't miss" collection of California gems, minerals, rocks, and fossils. Best of the gold-related exhibits are the 150-foot-long mine tunnel and the stamp mill and gold mine scale models. *Open daily except Tuesday, May through September; Wednesday through Sunday the rest of the year. Adults $3.50, seniors and teens $2.50, children under 14 free. Gift and book store.*

Lodging

Mariposa Hotel Inn

5029 Highway 140, at Charles Street
Mariposa, CA 95338
209/966-4676 **$$**

This cozy little refurbished inn (six rooms with baths) once served stage passengers. Enjoy a continental breakfast on the garden verandah.

Granny's Garden Bed & Breakfast

7333 Highway 49
Bear Valley, CA 95223
209/377-8342 **$$$**

Built around the turn of the century for a member of the pioneer Trabucco family (Granny), this Victorian farmhouse is still family-owned. Some of Granny's antiques decorate the two large suites. Guests enjoy a full breakfast, complimentary wine, and a spa.

Dining

Charles Street Dinner House

5043 Charles Street
Highway 140 and 7th Street
Mariposa
209/966-2366 **$$**

Much less formal than the name implies, this Old West-theme eatery is as popular with locals as tourists. The American cuisine is nicely prepared. *Dinner Wednesday through Sunday.*

Bon Ton Cafe

7307 Highway 49 North
Bear Valley
209/377-8228 **$**

This stone building—now housing a Mexican restaurant—was known as the Bon Ton Saloon in the 1800s. *Open for lunch and dinner Wednesday through Saturday, brunch and dinner Sunday.*

Mariposa County Courthouse   Photo courtesy of
Martin Litton

Side Trip

Hornitos

A rewarding 24-mile loop takes you to Hornitos, a one-time raucous, lawless town rich in history and colorful anecdotes. It was supposedly the favorite haunt of Joaquin Murieta, certainly the most storied outlaw of early California.

Founded by Mexican miners who had been voted out of neighboring Quartzburg by an American law-and-order committee, Hornitos reflects Mexican influence more than any other Gold Country settlement. (Incidentally, Quartzburg failed to survive despite its self-righteousness, or perhaps because of it.)

The town's name means "little ovens" in Spanish, and it was presumably named after the oven-shaped tombs that the first settlers built above the ground for their dead. Some of these unusual graves can still be seen in a fenced section of the little graveyard below St. Catherine's Church (built in 1862).

You can view Hornitos' first jail, a small building with 2-foot-thick granite walls, and the closed fronts of general stores, warehouses, and anonymous buildings that may once have been saloons, fandango halls, or gambling places. Some carry bullet holes from former gun battles. According to local report, one of the adobes on the west side of the main street at the north end of town was an opium den of considerable disrepute.

Across from the plaza are the remains of one of the first stores operated by D. Ghirardelli & Co., the well-known San Francisco chocolatier. Only the walls of the store, circa 1859, still stand.

Joaquin Murieta, a legendary bandit, was supposed to have used a secret tunnel at the corner of High Street and Bear Valley Road as an escape route from a fandango hall when circumstances got too hot. Contradicting this colorful tale is the practical contention that the tunnel was used to roll beer barrels from a cellar storeroom to the basement of the dance hall.

Hornitos' wild reputation has been enhanced by stories like that of the two gamblers (one version says they were women fandango dancers) who wrapped shirts (or shawls) around their arms as shields and duelled with gleaming knives until they killed each other in a vacant lot before a cheering audience of miners.

JOAQUIN MURIETA—
FABLE OR FACT?

Joaquin Murieta is certainly the California Gold Rush's most legendary figure. Immortalized in books, paintings, anecdotes, and even a Hollywood movie, Murieta emerged as the Robin Hood of the Southern Mines. He was the avenger of his murdered family, robber of the rich, friend to the poor, and defender of his countrymen. Visitors will find his name inscribed on historical markers and plaques throughout the region.

Saw Mill Flat, outside of Sonora, claims to be the place where Murieta first settled when he arrived from Sonora, Mexico, in 1850. It was in the town of Murphys that the handsome young man allegedly swore vengeance against Americans who persecuted Mexican miners. Supposedly a group of Yankees had tied him to a tree, beat him, ravished his wife, and murdered his brother.

San Andreas residents tell how a Frenchman made Murieta's famous bulletproof vest, and then had to prove its effectiveness by wearing it while Joaquin shot at him from point blank range. A tunnel in Hornitos was supposedly used by the bandit to escape lawmen. Joaquin is said to have hidden in a treehouse outside Volcano while puzzled rangers milled around beneath him. Mokelumne Hill and Sonora also claim to be the scenes of Murieta's wild escapades.

According to legend, Murieta died in 1853 when he was hunted down and shot to death in southern Mariposa County by a lawman named Harry Love. Love cut off the bandit's head, put it in a bottle of alcohol, and used it as proof to claim a reward.

How much of this is true? There are a few facts involved, but not many. In 1852 and 1853, the Southern Mines were bothered by a number of thieves, all seemingly named Joaquin. In response to public outcries the state legislature did hire Harry Love in May, 1853, to get a bandit named Joaquin—no last name specified—and offered $5,000 as a reward. Love didn't have much luck until he surprised a group of Mexicans around a campfire one night and killed a few, including an unnamed man who claimed to be their leader. Love decapitated the man, named him Joaquin Murieta, and went back to claim his reward.

The legislature paid off, but not everyone was convinced of the head's identity. A surviving member of the Mexican group claimed that it belonged to Joaquin Valenzuela. Those who "knew" Murieta stated that the grisly prize bore no resemblance to the man.

About a year after this confusion died down, the legend of Joaquin Murieta was born. Over the years, Joaquin grew more handsome, was able to trace his lineage to Montezuma, and displayed new tricks learned from his friend Kit Carson. The Gold Rush needed a romantic hero and, history aside, it seems that the legendary Joaquin Murieta will not die.

Coulterville

North of Bear Valley, Highway 49 coils into switchbacks as it makes a sinuous, thousand-foot descent into the Merced River gorge before slicing through what was once the town square of Coulterville. A turnout at the beginning of the grade provides panoramic views of the chasm once known as Hell's Hollow. The remains of Fremont's Pine Tree Mine can be seen about halfway down the hill. A side road over the bridge across the river leads to the Bagby Recreation Area, which offers camping and boating.

Coulterville sits snugly in a small valley at the junction of Highways 49 and 132, the latter an historic route to Yosemite Valley. Though its present population hovers around 100, at the height of the Gold Rush 5,000 miners (1,500 of whom were Chinese) filled 10 hotels and 25 saloons. Today just a few venerable buildings remain; others are only picturesque shells of stone and brick guarded by iron doors.

Photo courtesy of Martin Litton

Coulterville square is the home of "Whistling Billy", a locomotive that used to haul gold ore.

Rival merchants George W. Coulter and George Maxwell arrived at this Mexican mining camp at the same time, around 1849. The Mexicans called the American flag Coulter hoisted above his tent "Banderita" (little flag), and the camp acquired its first name. Ignoring this, however, Coulter and Maxwell drew lots to see which pioneer would have his name commemorated. Maxwell lost, but his name was later affixed to the nearby creek and the first post office.

Coulterville has been gutted by three fires. The third blaze in 1899 indirectly caused the village's last, and perhaps the country's shortest, "gold rush." Rubble from a stone-and-adobe building that was razed after the conflagration was used to fill chuckholes in the street. Apparently unknown to everyone living here, the walls of the building contained a secret cache of gold coins. With the first rain, several of these coins were exposed by the running water, and the rush was on. As the story goes, the town's populace turned out armed with shovels, picks, butcher knives, spoons, and other improbable mining tools, and quickly reduced the street to a state of impassable confusion.

The restored Hotel Jeffery on Main Street is the town's most imposing structure. Built in 1851, the two-story building originally housed a Mexican store and fandango hall. In 1870, it was converted to a hotel by George Jeffery. Ralph Waldo Emerson is only one of the famous—and infamous—who have stayed overnight.

Across the street are the remains of the Coulter Hotel and the Wells Fargo building that served as a trading post during the boom days. Nelson Cody, Buffalo Bill's brother, operated a trading post here during the 1870s and served as postmaster for many years. The structures now house the Northern Mariposa County History Center, a charming free museum stuffed with antiquities (open daily April to September except on Monday, weekends the rest of the year; closed in January).

In front of these buildings are the local "hangin' tree" and the small Whistling Billy steam engine. The engine was used at the rich Mary Harrison Mine to haul ore along a four-mile stretch of what was known as the world's crookedest railroad track. To see part of the foundation of the famous old mine that operated from the 1860s to 1903 and produced one and a half million dollars in gold, drive south about a mile on Highway 49 and turn right on the first black-topped road. The mine shaft was 1,200 feet deep, with 15 levels and 15 miles of drifts (tunnels).

Sun Sun Wo store (now an antique store), a remnant of one of the Gold Country's large Chinese settlements, is located on Chinatown Main Street and Kow Street on the town's east side. A private home next door to the 1851 adobe was formerly Candy's Place, a popular bordello.

Lodging

Hotel Jeffrey

P. O. Box 440
Coulterville, CA 95311
209/878-3471 $

Whether or not Teddy Roosevelt slept in this historic hotel is still debated, but Ralph Waldo Emerson certainly did. Refurbished in the 1980s, the historic hotel again serves travelers' eating and dining needs. Some of the 20 uptairs rooms have private baths; others are shared. The pleasant dining room is on the first floor and the old-time Magnolia Saloon is next door.

Big Oak Flat Detour

The Moccasin Creek Power Plant and Fish Hatchery at the junction of Highways 49 and 120 makes a good stop. (It's open weekdays only.) Highway 120 to the east climbs up Big Oak Flat past towns with historic pasts en route to Yosemite; to the west, the highway leads to Knights Ferry, where one of California's few remaining covered bridges spans the Stanislaus River.

The gold-laden gravels that made Big Oak Flat a rich placer camp were discovered late in 1849 by James Savage, whose company included five Native American wives and several servants. A year later, Savage became the first white man to explore Yosemite Valley.

Some weathered stone and adobe buildings and a monument are all that testify to the former boom town. Preserved in the monument are a few sections of wood from the large oak tree that gave the area its name. The tree fell when miners In their early frenzied search for gold reduced the gravels of the flat some five feet.

Charming Groveland, originally named Garrote in honor of the hanging of a horse thief in 1850, acquired its present name from a presumably calmer populace in the 1870s. Among the false-front buildings are the delightful Groveland Hotel, built in 1849, and the venerable Iron Door Saloon, which opened in 1852 and claims to be the state's oldest watering hole.

Up the road a few miles is Second Garrote, where some 60 men were said to have been hung during those violent days. An old cabin in the area was known as "Bret Harte's Cabin" and was supposedly the setting for his story, "Tennessee's Partner." Although the cabin burned years ago, the legend refuses to die.

Jason P. Chamberlain and John A. Chaffee, two young settlers who came to Second Garrote in 1852, might have been the models for the protagonists in Harte's tale. The men built a two-story frame house and lived as inseparable friends for the next 51 years. Long before Chaffee died in 1903, their reputation for loyalty to each other and kindness to travelers who passed along Big Oak Flat Road became a legend. Chamberlain lived on for three months after Chaffee's death, but finally, heartbroken and lonely, took his own life.

Lodging

Groveland Hotel

18767 Main Street; P.O. Box 289
Groveland, CA 95321
209/962-4000, (800)273-3314   **$$**

This beautifully restored hotel dates back to early Gold Rush days. Renovated in 1986, it has 17 cozy and comfortable rooms (private baths), a respected dining room, and conference facilities. During February and March, the hotel hosts mystery weekends, where guests participate in a 'whodunit' murder game.

Chinese Camp

One of the most famous and popular of the southern towns, Chinese Camp sits like an oasis amid grass and tarweed fields on Highway 49. There are some good ruins to explore, and one of the wildest fights ever staged in the foothills took place about three miles west of town.

No one really knows just where the Chinese who settled here came from. They may have been employed by English prospectors, or they could have been part of one of the many ship's crews that deserted in San Francisco during the early days of the Gold Rush. At any rate, there were no less than 5,000 Chinese mining here in the early 1850s.

Trouble arose in 1856, when, according to local history, a large stone rolled from the diggings of one group to an area where another group was working. A fight developed, and when it ended, the squabbling groups sent out a call for help to their respective tongs—the Sam Yap and Yan Wo. Each faction felt it had lost face and the only proper thing was to stage a full-scale war.

Chinese Camp church and graveyard   Photo courtesy of Martin Litton

Preparations were hurriedly made, and each side built up an arsenal of crude weapons. Local blacksmiths fashioned spears, tridents, battle axes, pikes, and daggers. A few muskets were brought from San Francisco, and Yankee miners were hired to instruct the combatants in the use of these strange instruments of destruction.

Finally all was ready. On October 25, 1856, 1,200 members of the Sam Yap fraternity met 900 Yan Wo brothers. Bolstered by speeches and some fire water, the two groups lined up and went for each other, hammer and tong. When the smoke cleared, four people were dead—most likely trampled to death—and another dozen were injured. About 250 were taken prisoner by local American law authorities. The war was over, stature regained, and everybody went back to the mines.

Jamestown

About a mile south of Jamestown, Highway 49 crosses Woods Creek, site of the discovery of a 75-pound nugget. Tuolumne County's first strike, in August of 1848, was made at Woods Creek. It's said more gold was taken from the creek than from any other stream its size in California. For a time miners were digging out $200 to $300 a day with a pick and knife.

Mining tunnels honeycomb most of Table Mountain, an ancient lava mass roughly a quarter-mile wide and 40 miles long; take Rawhide Road for a good view. The Humbug Mine, on the mountain's eastern slope, yielded some $4 million in gold and nuggets the size of hen's eggs.

Weekend prospecting still goes on along area creeks, and a large open pit mine is operated commercially nearby. In 1984, construction workers laying a sewer line uncovered some small nugggets in the trench; within minutes, locals bought every gold pan in town and started digging it out faster than the crew could fill it.

Jamestown was founded in 1848 by Col. George James, a lawyer from San Francisco not known for his scruples. After disgruntled citizens forced James to leave town, they tried to change the settlement's name to American Camp, but "Jimtown" was too firmly fixed to be legislated out of existence.

Hollywood likes Jimtown: it's appeared as a backdrop in such movies as High Noon and Butch Cassidy and the Sundance Kid. The town tries valiantly to retain its look of antiquity, even though many of its original wood-frame buildings were destroyed by fire in 1966. Some structures from the 1870s and 1880s and some fire-resistant blockhouses dating from the 1850s still stand. The ones on Main Street house antique shops and stores selling gold in many forms. The fancy gingerbread and brick Emporium and the Community Methodist Church are among the most photogenic survivors.

Photo courtesy of the Golden Chain Council

Jamestown, called "an oasis of antiquity" by the local community, features Railtown 1897 State Historic Park.

Historic Attractions

Railtown 1897 State Historic Park

Three blocks from the intersection
of Highways 49 and 108
P.O. Box 1250
Jamestown, CA 95327
209/984-3953

Modest admission to grounds. Gift shop and picnic area. When the state acquired the historic Sierra Railway property, rail buffs and children fascinated with trains gained a chance to see everything needed to run a railroad—steam engines, rail cars, depot, yards, roundhouse, and track. Happily, the property looks much as it did at the turn of the century when the tracks first reached Jamestown.

One of the line's original locomotives (built in 1891) is its star performer, the much-photographed Old No. 3, a 4-6-0 Rogers. It was the Hooter Cannonball of Petticoat Junction fame and, along with other Sierra Railway locomotives, has starred in some 200 movies, television shows, and commercials. *Guided roundhouse tours daily year-round; steam train rides on weekends and holidays, March through November.*

Diversions

Gold panning

Gold Prospecting Expeditions
18170 Main Street, Jamestown

Columbia Mining and Equipment
18169 Main Street, Jamestown

Get the hang of gold panning at horse troughs in front of these two stores, or sign up for longer outings at nearby streams.

Lodging

Jamestown Hotel

18153 Main Street
Jamestown, CA 95327
209/984-3902 **$$**

This two-story brick charmer with its false-front facade and wooden verandah has eight upstairs rooms complete with Victorian furnishings and baths. Downstairs are a public dining room and a cozy saloon noted for its antique back bar.

National Hotel

77 Main Street, Jamestown
CA 95327
209/984-3446 **$$**

Dating from 1859, this handsomely restored hostelry is one of the Mother Lode's oldest continuously operating hotels. Five of the 11 rooms have private baths (brass pull-chain toilets); the other six share two large baths. Guests enjoy continental breakfast in the dining room or garden courtyard. Visitors and locals mingle at the redwood bar.

Dining

Michelangelo

18228 Main Street
Jamestown
209/984-4830 **$**

Full bar. Contemporary Italian cuisine and decor make this eatery a popular choice with townfolk and visitors. *Open for dinner Wednesday through Monday.*

Smoke Cafe

18191 Main Street
Jamestown
209/984-3733 **$**

Southwestern decor combines with nouvelle Mexican fare. *Open for dinner Tuesday through Sunday. Bar and patio.*

Sonora

An attractive setting and a great deal of history behind a modern facade makes Sonora a good base camp for enjoying much of the colorful surrounding countryside. The historic downtown area is best explored on foot. Traffic on its narrow main street (Washington) crawls along for several blocks past aged buildings housing cafes and small shops.

In the early 1850s, Sonora and nearby Columbia battled it out for preeminence. Today there is no question about which is the liveliest. As the seat of Tuolumne County, a trading center for surrounding cattle and lumber country, and a gateway to the Sierra Nevada high country, Sonora is as busy today as it was more than a century ago.

Sonora's early history was marred by some ugly incidents between Mexicans and Yankees. The town originally was settled early in 1848 by Mexicans and was known as Sonorian Camp. But the gringos weren't far behind, and they did their best to drive off the settlers from the south. A vindictive $20-a-month state tax on foreigners was aimed principally at Mexican miners, causing the latter to band together in defiance.

Though there was scattered violence, the Mexicans soon realized they were beaten and left town in a mass exodus, causing Sonora's population to drop from 5,000 to 3,000 practically overnight. The business community suffered hard times until the tax was repealed in 1851 and Mexicans once again felt it safe to return.

The Big Bonanza Mine, believed to be the biggest pocket mine ever found in the Mother Lode, was located on Piety Hill near the north end of Washington Street. First worked by Chileans, who took out a large amount of surface gold, it was purchased for a pittance by three partners in the 1870s. After several years of patient work they broke through into a body of almost solid gold. Within one day they sent $160,000 worth of gold to the San Francisco mint, and within a week another $500,000 was shipped.

During its peak production, Sonora was known as the Queen of the Southern Mines—and one of the wildest towns in the foothills. The main street was lined haphazardly with buildings made of adobe, hewn planks, sailcloth, and tin. Horse races and bull-and-bear fights were common, and there was no lack of painted ladies. Liquid refreshment was readily available at any hour of the day or night.

Historic Attractions

Tuolumne County Museum and History Center

158 W. Bradford Avenue
Sonora
209/532-1317

You can pick up a copy of a walking tour of heritage homes and other points of interest (don't overlook the impressive cemetery on Yaney Street) at the Tuolumne County Museum and History Center. Housed in a century-old jail, the museum displays a gold collection that chronicles the area's mining history. Several restored cells contain exhibits; a former exercise yard is a picnic area. *Open Tuesday through Saturday from 10 A.M. to 4 P.M. year-round. Donations encouraged.*

St. James Episcopal Church

North Washington and Snell streets, Sonora

Unquestionably the outstanding piece of old architecture in Sonora, this striking, dark red church was built in 1860. It's not the oldest structure in the Gold Country, but it's certainly the most beautiful frame building. The rectory has a museum (open weekdays) detailing the history of the Red Church. The Street-Morgan Mansion across the street, an elegant Victorian painted to match the church, now serves as business offices.

St. James Episcopal Church   Photo courtesy of Martin Litton

Lodging

Gunn House

286 S. Washington Street
Sonora
209/532-3421 $

This historic two-story adobe, now operating as an inn, was built by Dr. Lewis C. Gunn in 1850. Originally it served as a residence for his family. It later became the offices for the Sonora Herald, the first newspaper in the mining area. The inn offers 28 rooms of varying charm and a swimming pool.

Ryan House, 1855

153 S. Shepherd Street
Sonora, CA 95370
209/533-3445 **$$**

Built as a residence by the Ryan family who came here in 1855 from Ireland to escape the potato famine, this little gem has been transformed into a picture-pretty inn with three rooms. Breakfast in the rose garden is a treat.

Serenity

15305 Bear Cub Drive
Sonora, CA 95370
six miles east of downtown
off Phoenix Lake Road
209/533-1441 **$$**

Touches of yesterday combine with comforts of today at this oasis: four cheerfully decorated rooms, a wraparound deck for wildlife watching, a library crammed with books and games, plus a breakfast fit for gourmets.

Oak Hill Ranch

P.O. Box 307
Tuolumne, CA 95379
18550 Connally Lane
off Apple Colony Road
209/928-4717 **$$**

A quintessential B&B east of Sonora at the 3,000-foot; level, this Victorian replica offers five bedrooms, a wealth of antiques, a private pond, and lavish beakfasts.

Sonora Oaks Motor Hotel

19551 Hess Avenue
Sonora, CA 95370
209/533-4400 **$$**

This two-story motel in a quiet setting off Highway 49 is among Sonora's newest and best lodgings. It has 70 modern rooms, a pool, and a restaurant.

Dining

Hemingway's

362 S. Stewart Street
Sonora
209/532-4900 **$$**

Papa's memorabilia gives this bistro its name. A garden setting, California contemporary cuisine, and music on weekends make it popular with Sonorans. *Open for lunch Tuesday through Friday, dinner Tuesday through Sunday.*

Columbia State Historic Park

When gold was being extracted at a record pace in the 1850s, the town of Columbia was known as the Queen of the Southern Mines. It deserves equally high billing today, not for its gold but for its unparalleled collection of reconstructed buildings and mining artifacts. It's also a good starting point for anyone interested in exploring the state's golden past.

You can pick up a sizable fund of knowledge here about architecture and miners' habits that will help you figure out the sometimes confusing ruins and deserted camps located elsewhere. Every building is clearly identified. In addition, there is an abundance of maps, guide books, and souvenirs that go to great lengths to explain history and current attractions in detail.

The free park is open daily year-round from 8 A.M. to 6 P.M. Most of the activities are offered daily from Memorial Day to Labor Day and on weekends the rest of the year. For more information, call (209) 532-0150.

Columbia ranked as the largest town in the Southern Mines during its heyday. Some 15,000 people lived here when the earth was giving up a fortune, estimated at $87 million. The town rang with the clamor of hectic activity and the shouts and curses of thousands of miners, gamblers, merchants, dance hall girls, and miscellaneous camp followers who always managed to thrive in most successful camps. Stagecoaches rattled into town every day, and the roads were crowded with freight wagons bringing in new provisions and merchandise from Stockton.

Gold was discovered here in 1850 by Dr. Thaddeus Hildreth. First called Hildreth's Diggings, then American Camp, the settlement was formally christened Columbia at the time of its incorporation in 1852. It was known for its energetic citizens, but also had its share of violence and brutality.

After it caught fire a number of times, including a disastrous blaze in 1854, Columbia was rebuilt with brick, fireproof doors, and iron shutters—one reason for the pretty much intact town

Photo courtesy of Martin Litton

Columbia, one of the most important settlements in the Gold Country, was known as the "Gem of the Southern Mines."

you see today. Restorations increase steadily as funds become available.

Historic Attractions

For best use of your time, stop by park headquarters (Main and State streets) for a walking tour map, then visit the William Cavalier Museum for an overview of the Gold Rush, including exhibits, slide shows, and films.

Columbia is much more than a collection of restored buildings. This is still a living community, albeit tourist-oriented. Students enrolled in Hospitality Management Program at the local Columbia College staff and operate the City Hotel and Fallon House.

Tourists can enjoy panning for "color" down in Matelot Gulch, riding the jouncing stagecoach from the Wells Fargo office through the granite-ribbed hills behind town, selecting a horse from a corral near the Miner's Shack, sipping sarsaparilla at the Douglass or St. Charles saloons, watching the "smithy" at work, or getting a haircut at the state's oldest barber shop. There's Hangtown Fry or some other '49er delicacy to sample in restaurants, sweets from the Candy Kitchen, and freshly baked cones at the ice cream parlor.

St. Anne's Catholic Church perches atop Kennebec Hill south of town. Probably the first brick church in California (1856), St. Anne's overlooks the world's richest placer grounds. In the old cemetery, notice the number of Spanish, French, and Italian names on the marble headstones.

A climb up a hill at the town's north end leads to a two-story brick schoolhouse built in 1860 and restored 100 years later. School children from all over the state contributed funds for this restoration of one of the state's earliest public schools. Signs call attention to the attractions along a short nature trail named for a local teacher.

You can sign up at the Miner's Shack for a tour of an operating quartz mine on Italian Bar Road. Tours are offered daily in summer, and on weekends the rest of the year.

Diversions

Fallon House Theatre

209/532-4644

A talented repertory troupe presents a variety of family fare, including dramas, comedies, musicals, and melodramas during the summer season. *Scheduled performances 8 P.M. Thursday through Saturday, 2 P.M. Sunday*

Lodging

City Hotel Main Street

Between Jackson and State streets
P.O. Box 1870
Columbia, CA 95310
209/532-1479 **$$**

This lovingly restored period piece is a hotel and hospitality training center for Columbia College students. Six of the 10 rooms open off the upstairs parlor, which is the setting for the continental breakfast included with room rental. Rooms include half-baths plus robes and toiletry baskets for the trek to the showers down the hall. The hotel's noted restaurant (see next page) and What Cheer bar are downstairs.

Fallon House

Washington Street off Broadway
P.O. Box 1870
Columbia, CA 95310
209/532-1470 **$$**

Restored in 1988 to an elegant 1890s splendor, this building's early incarnations included courthouse, bakery, and rooming house. Staff of the hotel are college hospitality trainees. The 14-room inn has one room with full bath; the others have half-baths. Complementary robes and toiletries ease the trip to the showers. Rates include complementary breakfast.

Dining

City Hotel Restaurant

*Main Street between Jackson
and State streets, Columbia
(209) 532-1479* **$$$**

The esteemed restaurant in the nicely renovated hotel offers both a *prix fixe* dinner menu and *à la carte* suggestions for continental-style dining. Costumed servers are from the area's Columbia College. *Open for dinner Tuesday through Sunday, Sunday brunch. Reservations required weekends, recommended rest of week.*

Side Trip

North to Jackass Hill

A marker at the small town of Tuttletown on Highway 49 is fashioned of stones from Swerer's store, where Bret Harte was a clerk and Mark Twain was a customer. Jackass Hill, about a mile north, got its name from the braying of the hundreds of mules tied up here overnight when pack trains stopped to rest. The main attraction now is a reconstruction of a cabin where Mark Twain lived for five months as the guest of William and James Gillis. While visiting, he researched and wrote serveral stories, including a tale of a jumping frog in Angels Camp.

Photo courtesy of Tuolumne County Visitors Bureau

Camping site at Don Pedro Lake

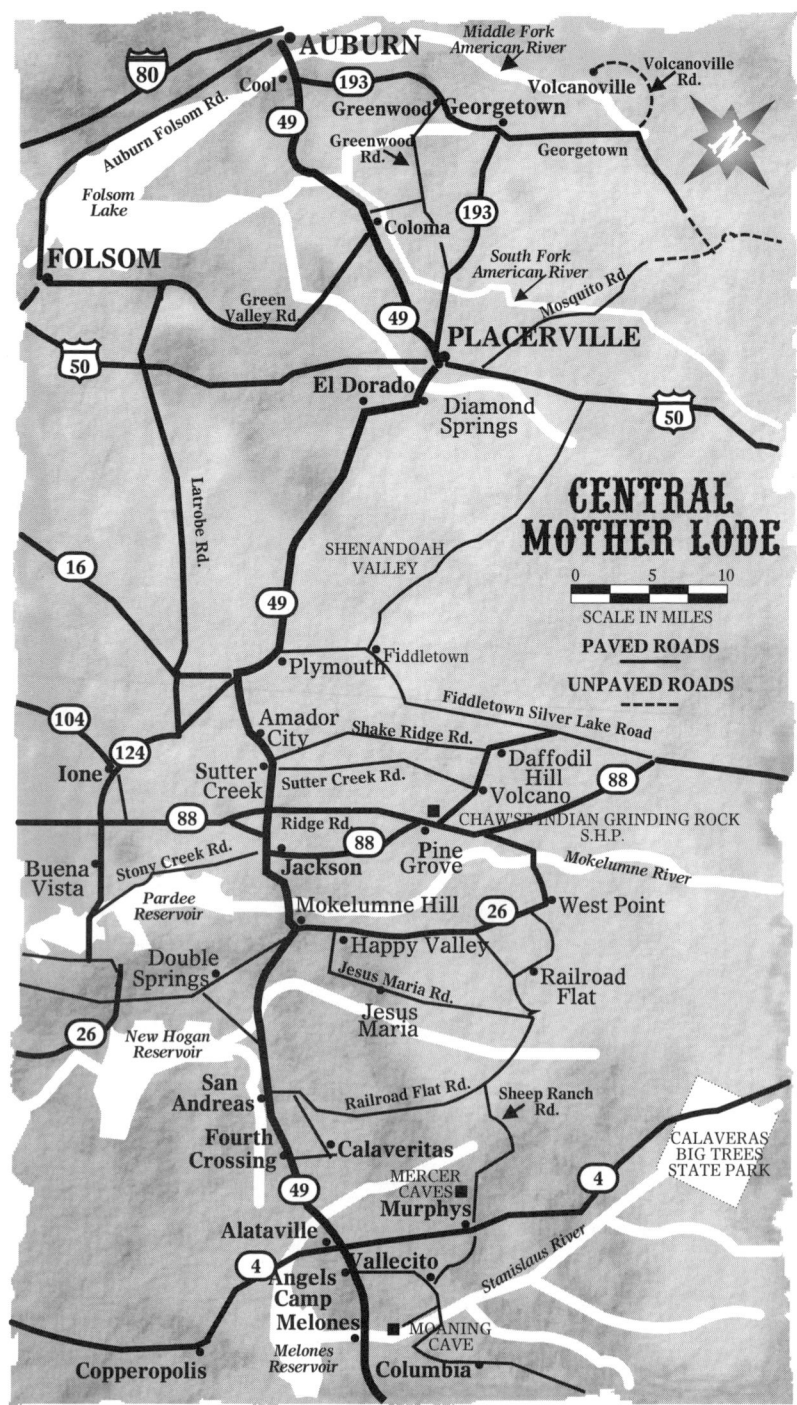

CENTRAL MOTHER LODE

Much of California's Gold Country was called the Mother Lode, but the section between Melones to the south and Auburn to the north contained the primary gold vein that gave the area its name. This region had the deepest, and some of the richest, mines, and is the most-visited part of the Gold Country. It retains a surprising number of relatively intact historical towns and buildings.

Travelers will find a variety of accommodations, ranging from old inns to modern motels and restaurants. A large number of colorful annual events are held in this area, including the crowd-drawing Jumping Frog Contest. Here too are facilities for a wealth of year-round family recreational activities—fishing, boating, swimming, and skiing.

Angels Camp

South of Angels Camp on Highway 49 is Carson Hill, considered in its heyday to be the richest of all the Mother Lode camps. Together, the consolidated mines of Carson Hill and Melones produced over $26 million in gold. Topping the big nuggets taken from this area was one 15 inches long, six inches wide, and four inches thick. It weighed 195 pounds and was worth about $43,000 in those days, about $2 million today.

Between Carson Hill and Angels Camp stands a lonely stone house that is slowly but steadily falling victim to the elements. This is the Romaggi home, the only remnant of Albany Flat. James

Romaggi arrived from Genoa in 1850; scorning gold, he built this house and planted vineyards and orchards, establishing one of the finest ranches in the Mother Lode. The stretch of road on either side of the house was once lined with buildings, but, when drought killed the vines and trees, Albany Flat faded from sight.

Thanks to Mark Twain, Angels Camp is probably better noted for frogs than for its Gold Rush background, but a few historical remembrances still exist. Pick up a walking tour guide at the Calaveras Visitor Center (1301 Main Street).

In 1928, the city fathers decided to celebrate their street paving by staging a frog jump in honor of Twain's story, The Celebrated Jumping Frog of Calaveras County. The idea was so good—and so entertaining—that frog jumping has become an international event held annually the third weekend of May during the Calaveras County Fair. The monument to the frog along the highway far outshadows the statue of Twain in shady Utica Park.

The bustling little town takes its name from George Angel, a member of the 7th Regiment of New York Volunteers who came west in 1848 and founded a trading post where Angels Creek and Dry Creek come together. The camp grew rapidly during the 1850s, and, although the setting was changed, it was probably the place Bret Harte wrote about in Luck of Roaring Camp.

The story of the discovery of the quartz lode which made Angels Camp one of the greatest mining centers in the Mother Lode is often told. It seems a miner named Rasberry (for whom Rasberry Lane was named) was having difficulty with his muzzle-loading rifle one day. The ramrod had jammed and in a moment of exasperation he fired the rifle into the ground. When he went to retrieve the ramrod, which had shot out and struck the ground, he found a piece of rock that had broken from the impact and glittered with what was unmistakably gold. Rasberry took almost $10,000 from the new claim in three days, and went on to make a fortune following the vein.

VOICES OF THE WEST

Bret Harte and Mark Twain are the most famous and most popular of the many writers who used California's Gold Rush for inspiration, background, and characters. Their writings did as much to inform the world of the unique qualities of the Gold Rush as any history book ever could.

Bret Harte

Bret Harte was only 12 years old when gold was discovered at Coloma and only 18 when he came to California in 1854 to join his mother and stepfather in Oakland. Yearning for adventure, he spent two months in 1855 wandering around mining camps from Angels Camp south. He taught school for a time in La Grange and then moved on to Robinson's Ferry on the Stanislaus River. Wherever he went, he was welcomed by superstitious miners who believed that a tenderfoot always brought luck.

Mark Twain

By his own admission, Harte never really got to know the towns or the people intimately during his short stay in the Gold Rush Country. He was always the dude, wearing boiled shirts and patent leather shoes, and keeping his distance from the intimacies of mining life. He didn't like the Sierra foothills, asserting that they were "hard, ugly, unwashed, vulgar, and lawless."

Harte later embarked on a series of successful careers: printer, newspaperman, magazine editor and writer. He eventually returned to the East, abandoning California but never turning his back on the West as a subject for his writing. Many of his best stories–even those written when he was living in England after 1885–dealt with frontiersmen and life in the mining towns.

Samuel Clemens was born in Missouri in 1835 (a year before Harte) but did not come West until 1861, when he accompanied his brother Orion, the newly appointed secretary of the Nevada territory. By that time, he had served as a reporter, printer, Mississippi River pilot, and even a Confederate soldier for two weeks at the start of the Civil War.

Young Sam tried prospecting in Nevada, then worked as city editor of the Virginia City Enterprise, where he first used the pseudonym of Mark Twain in 1862. He moved to San Francisco in 1864, and there met Bret Harte, who was a great help in getting "Twain stories" published and in improving the author's style.

In December, 1864, Twain visited the Gillis brothers, who had been kind to Bret Harte a few years earlier. They tried pocket mining for a time and spent a lot of time in Angels Camp during the inclement weather. It was on a cold January day that Twain heard an old Mississippi River pilot named Ben Coon relate a funny anecdote about a frog-jumping contest. A few months later, Twain wrote The Celebrated Jumping Frog of Calaveras County and became an overnight literary sensation. Though he left California the next year, he had collected enough material to last him for many years.

Twain made it a point to learn the miners' habits and trade. He once said, "I know the mines and miners interiorly as well as Bret Harte knows them exteriorly." That was the major difference between the two. Harte had a genius for the narrative and could capture character and local color in just a few words. But his stories lacked depth and were those of an outsider. Twain, on the other hand, wrote like he talked, with a vitality that more truly reflected the California frontier and the rough people who settled it.

The two famous voices of the West were silenced within a few years of each other. Twain died in Connecticut in 1910; Harte in England in 1902.

Jumping Frog Jubilee, the Calaveras County Fair, Angels Camp

Historic Attraction

Angels Camp Museum

753 S. Main Street
Angels Camp
209/735-2963

Among the nicely organized collection of early-day artifacts on display at this city museum are mining equipment, wagons, a carriage house, and a working scale model of the stamp mill used at the Carson Hill Mine. *Open daily 10 A.M. to 3 P.M. from April to Thanksgiving, Wednesday through Sunday the rest of the year; closed major holidays. Nominal admission.*

Side Trip

Altaville to Copperopolis

Altaville stands at the junction of Highways 4 and 49. A busy little burg (named Forks in the Road when it was settled in 1852), Altaville was the site of California's first iron foundry in 1854. Of note is the handsome old Prince and Garibardi store, a well-preserved, two-story stone building erected in 1857.

Altaville's name perhaps is best known in connection with the Gold Country's greatest hoax. It was from a mine in nearby Bald Mountain that a human skull, soon to be known as the Pliocene Skull, was taken in 1866 and presented to the scientific world as the remains of a prehistoric man. The argument over the skull's authenticity continued for over 50 years, until it was finally decided that the skull was actually Native American in origin and had been placed at the bottom of the mine shaft as an ambitious—and successful—practical joke.

Bret Harte's poem "To the Pliocene Skull" captures the ridiculous aspects of the whole affair. Strangely, no one connected with the joke ever revealed his part.

Following Highway 4 west leads through Copperopolis. As its name implies, the town was one of the few in the area founded on a mineral other than gold. During the Civil War, it was one of the country's principal copper-producing centers, boasting a population of several thousand people from 1860 to 1867.

Some of the town's old buildings were built in the 1860s of brick hauled from Columbia, where perfectly good stores were being torn down by miners to get at the gold-rich soil underneath the foundations. At the south end of town are three notable structures, the largest of which served as headquarters for the Copperopolis Blues during the Civil War.

Murphys

Tall locust trees line the streets of this grand old town nine miles east of Angels Camp. In their shade life goes on much as it has through the decades since the Gold Rush ended. In its beautiful setting, Murphys is one of the most charming towns in the Mother Lode and an ideal place to take a casual stroll and soak up the atmosphere.

Murphys is most quickly reached by Highway 4. To make a loop trip, travelers can then return via Murphys Grade Road, rejoining Highway 49 at Altaville.

On Highway 4, you pass through Vallecito, which still has two Gold Rush mementos: the Dinkelspiel store and Wells Fargo Express office. An interesting story is told about the school at nearby Douglas Flat. It is said that because the building was located on gold-bearing gravel, part of the teacher's salary was the right to pan for gold during recess.

Murphys was first settled in July, 1848, by John and Daniel Murphy, who came west in 1844 with the first wagon train to cross the Sierra Nevada. By 1849, the Murphys made their fortune and left town. But others stayed, prospered, and erected the substantial brick and limestone buildings that you see today.

The building across from the Murphys Hotel (see below) started life as a bakery and miners' supply store. Farther east, another brick-fronted building with the legend "Stephens Bros. Cheap Cash" painted across the side was, at an earlier time, Jones' Apothecary Shop. St. Patrick's Catholic Church, built in 1858, is considered one of the best examples of early construction techniques.

Historic Attractions

Old Timers Museum

472 Main Street
Murphys

The structure in which this small museum is housed is known as the Peter Traver building. One of its exterior walls honors Gold Country notables and the achievements of the E Clampus Vitus fraternal lodge. Built in 1856, it's the oldest building in Murphys, having survived three fires. *Open Thursday through Sunday; weekends only in winter. Donations.*

Calaveras Big Trees State Park

P.O. Box 120
Arnold, CA 95223
209/795-2334

Camping, hiking, picnicking, swimming, fishing in the North Fork of the Stanislaus River in summer; cross-country skiing in winter. This large stand of Sequoiadendron giganteum (over 6,000 acres) lies about 20 miles northeast of Murphys on Hghway 4. The Big Trees were first seen by John Bidwell on a scouting expedition in 1841. Credit for their discovery, however, is usually given to A.T. Dowd, a hunter from Murphys, who brought them to public attention in 1852.

Photo courtesy of Martin Litton
Murphys Hotel, Murphys, Caleveras County

FRATERNAL LODGES

One thing that visitors to the Gold Country note is the large number of lodge halls still standing. An I.O.O.F. or Masonic hall is frequently the most conspicuous building in town, and a reflection of an important Gold Rush phenomenon—the need for companionship.

The Odd Fellows and the Masons were among the strong fraternal organizations in the East who sanctioned California lodges early in 1849 to help any brethren who might encounter trouble far from home. New lodges opened with each new strike. Organizers had little trouble recruiting members, since miners lept at every chance to help overcome their lonely life. Those who struck it rich gave freely to building campaigns, with the result that the lodge halls were made of stone and brick while many other buildings were wood and canvas.

There was one fraternity that didn't quite fit this mold. E Clampus Vitus was founded in 1850 by J. H. Zumwalt of Mokelumne Hill, a man of good humor who decided that the solemn and mysterious fraternal organizations could do with a bit of needling. The "task" of E Clampus Vitus was to take care of widows and orphans ("mostly widows"). Members were all held in an office of equal indignity and were ruled by a Noble Grand Humbug. Pledged to a life of jollity and informality, the brethren developed such a comradely spirit that a man would have a hard time doing business in many communities if he were not a member.

Despite all the partying and joking, the Clampers managed to do some good deeds by helping the needy. The charity was always anonymous, but the many letters of thanks printed in newspapers of the day attest to the regard in which the pranksters were held.

E Clampus Vitus was revived in the 1930s, and several historical markers erected by modern Clampers can be spottted throughout the Gold Country. An exterior wall of the Old Timers Museum building in Murphys commemorates some of the early members.

Diversions

Spelunking

Area visitors have three chances to enter the underground world. Caverns are open daily in summer (Moaning Cavern is open daily year-round) and some weekends the rest of the year. Moderate admissions are charged.

Mercer Caverns (209/728-2101), one mile north of Murphys off Sheep Ranch Road, was discovered by Walter Mercer in 1885. Looking for water on a hot September day, he sat down in the shade. A force of cold air on his legs led him to the cave entrance, which he excavated and opened to the public in 1887. Tours take groups through a series of galleries filled with dramatic formations. The temperature inside is a constant 55 degrees.

Moaning Cavern (209/736-2708), two miles south of Vallecito off Parrotts Ferry Road, was discovered by miners in 1851. Part of the fun is getting into this vertical cave: you either descend by a series of wooden stairs before reaching a spiral steel staircase, or you rappel from the surface into the large main chamber (extra charge). The staircase, added in 1922, unfortunately spoiled the acoustics for which the cavern was named.

California Caverns (209/736-2708), 12 miles east of San Andreas off Mountain Ranch Road, were discovered by a prospector in 1849, and opened to the public the following year. If you have time for only one cave tour, this is a good bet. Signatures from 1850s spelunkers are still visible on the walls. Guided tours of the extensive caverns are offered daily. Spelunking and rappelling trips are available by reservation.

Wine touring

The argonauts who poured in during the Gold Rush were soon followed by winemakers. By the 1870s, Calaveras County ranked among the country's top wine-producing regions. In the 1970s viticulture began to make a small comeback, and six wineries around Murphys show you why the region's wines are so well regarded. Pack a picnic and enjoy tasting some of the vintages.

Black Sheep Vintners
342 French Gulch Road
Murphys
209/728-2157
Open weekend afternoons

Chatom Vineyards
1969 Highway 4
Douglas Flat
209/736-6500
Open daily 11 A.M. to 4:30 P.M.
Picnic area

Indian Rock Vineyards
1154 Pennsylvania Gulch Road
Murphys
209/728-2266
Open 11 A.M. to 5 P.M. weekends

Kautz Ironstone Vineyards
Six Mile Road, Murphys
209/728-1251
Open 11 A.M. to 5 P.M. daily
Guided tours; deli and beautifully-landscaped picnic sites

Milliaire Winery
276 Main Street
Murphys
209/728-1658
Open 11 A.M. to 4:30 P.M. daily

Stevenot Winery
2690 San Domingo Road
Murphys
209/728-3436
Open 10 A.M.to 5 P.M. daily

Lodging

Cooper House Bed and Breakfast Inn

1184 Church Street
P.O. Box 1388
Angels Camp, CA 95222
209/736-2145 **$$**

This Craftsman-style bungalow with its quiet garden setting was once home to the town's physician. Rates for the three suites (each named for a grape variety) include a full breakfast.

Dunbar House, 1880

271 Jones Street
P.O. Box 1375
Murphys, CA 95247
209/728-2897 **$$**

In a lovely garden setting, this large Italianate inn offers four rooms, all with private baths. Enjoy the included breakfast in your room, the dining room, or the garden.

Murphys Hotel

457 Main Street
P.O. Box 329
Murphys, CA 95247
209/728-3444 **$**

Refurbished nine-room hostelry (shared baths) and 20-room modern motel. Dining room and saloon. Murphys' most prominent structure is the hotel built by James Sperry and John Perry in 1855 to accommodate the growing number of visitors passing through on their way to view the newly discovered Big Trees. Examining the old register, you find names of past travelers: Mark Twain, U.S. Grant, Henry Ward Beecher, Thomas Lipton (of tea fame), J. Pierpont Morgan, Horatio Alger, and many others. No one would ever have taken the quiet signer of the entry "Charles Bolton, Silver Mountain" for the notorious stagecoach robber, Black Bart.

Redbud Inn

402 Main Street
Murphys, CA 95247
209/728-8533 **$$**

Murphys newest lodging offers 12 luxuriously furnished, individually decorated rooms and baths in the Miner's Exchange Complex. Breakfast and evening hors d'oeuvres are included in the rate; massages and herbal baths (by appointment) are extra.

Dining

Murphys Hotel

Address on previoius page **$**

The dining room of this hotel is tucked away behind the bar. Standard American dishes often receive an innovative twist.

San Andreas

Highway realignments and other demands of modern civilization have stripped San Andreas of most of its mining camp character and left only a few original Gold Rush buildings along Main Street: the dressed-stone Fricot Building, the ubiquitous I.O.O.F. Hall, and the old courthouse, which houses part of the county museum (see below). Behind the courthouse is the old jail with a cell marked prominently "Black Bart slept here."

Just west of town is the historic Pioneer Cemetery, dating back at least to 1851. Most of the graves are unmarked, but the few headstones still standing have very intriguing inscriptions. Many graves were moved here when Camanche Lake inundated the mining towns of Lancha Plana, Camanche, and Poverty Bar.

A century ago rich gravels yielded gold to the Mexican miners who settled the town in 1849, then to Yankees who crowded them out in 1850, and finally to thousands of Chinese who had the patience to rework tailings considered uesless by others.

BLACK BART–
HIGHWAYMAN

Black Bart was credited with 28 stagecoach robberies between 1877 and 1883, and stage drivers throughout northern California lived in dread of the day when Bart would step out of the brush in some secluded ravine and call out politely, "Will you please throw down your treasure box, sir?"

Bart's character and habits were just as interesting as his *modus operandi* as a bandit. He dressed in a long linen duster and wore a flour sack over his head with holes cut out for the eyes. He was always on foot and carried only a shotgun and a blanket roll in which he tucked an axe for breaking open the strongboxes. Bart chose his locations carefully, and always waited for the coaches at sharp bends in the road where the horses would be moving at a walk.

He was gentle with his victims and never harmed drivers or passengers. It was revealed later that he never owned a single shell for his shotgun and could not have fired it even in self-defense. Bart earned the reputation as a poet by leaving bits of doggerel at the scenes of two early robberies. He signed the poetry as "Black Bart, the PO8 (po-ate)."

Bart's colorful career came to an end when he was wounded escaping from a holdup near Copperopolis, and accidentally dropped a handkerchief with the laundry mark "FX07." The mark was traced Charles E. Bolton, a customer of a San Francisco laundry. Much to everyone's surprise, Bolton and Black Bart were one and the same.

After his arrest, Bolton confessed to the crimes and told a strange tale of his life as a westernized *Dr. Jekyll and Mr. Hyde.* He was born in Illinois as Charles E. Boles and grew up as an intelligent, well-educated citizen. After serving in the Civil War, he emigrated to California in search of gold. Unable to find any legally, Boles decided to try his hand at highwaymanship. He clerked for a time in several stage offices to study shipments and schedules. Then in August, 1877, he transformed himself into Black Bart and made his first holdup.

With success came prosperity. He took the name of Bolton, and quickly built a reputation as a non-smoking, non-drinking, God-fearing man with big business interests in the mines. He was seen frequently in prominent social circles, always nattily dressed and wearing fancy jewelry. When more cash was needed to support his lifestyle, he would go to the foothills and knock over a convenient stage.

Black Bart's fascinating life did not end with his arrest. During his trial in San Andreas, the newspapers made him a legend by exaggerating his exploits, ballooning the size of his ill-gotten gains, and grossly exaggerating his talent at "PO8try." Amid much publicity, Bart was convicted and sentenced to six years at San Quentin prison.

After his release, Bart stayed around San Francisco for a while. But early in 1888, he left for the San Joaquin Valley where he quietly disappeared into the dusty heat. The last verified report found him in Visalia and moving. For a time, there was a rumor that Wells Fargo had pensioned the old man and sent him away after he agreed not to rob any more stages. That, too, is in the realm of legend, and no one will ever know for sure just what finally happened to the honorable Charles E. Boles (alias Bolton and Black Bart), the most famous stage robber of Gold Rush history.

Historic Attraction

Calaveras County Museum and Archives

30 N. Main Street
San Andreas
209/754-6579

Three buildings—I.O.O.F. Hall, Hall of Records, and Court-house—make up this comprehensive collection of county history from the days of the Miwoks through the Gold Rush and beyond. *Museum open daily 10 A.M. to 4 P.M. except major holidays. Small admission.*

Lodging

Robin's Nest

247 W. Charles Street, P.O. Box 1408
San Andreas, CA 95249
209/754-1076 $$

One of the town's most attractive residences, this century-old Queen Anne Victorian has nine rooms and baths. The tub in the Snyder Suite is seven-feet-long. A bountiful breakfast is included in the rate.

Side Trip

Calaveritas

A winding side road, roughly parallel to and several miles east of Highway 49, affords an alternate route between Altaville and San Andreas. Curving Dogtown Road (which turns into Calaveritas Road) passes through the sites of the former colorfully named mining camps of Dogtown, Calaveritas, Scratch Gulch, and Brandy Flat. Only at Calaveritas is there any tangible evidence of this once-flourishing gold area. Formerly a settlement of stores, saloons, and fandango halls (where it is said bandit Joaquin Murieta was a frequent visitor), Calaveritas was destroyed by fire in 1858. A few buildings, including the old Costa store (on private property), still stand as mute testimony to a more turbulent time.

Mokelumne Hill

Photogenic "Mok Hill" has an attractive setting, good collection of early architecture, and an unmistakable mountain-type ambience. Many buildings are made of a light-brown stone known as rhyolite tuff, a material common to much of the Mother Lode. Best-known reminders of Gold Rush days are the I.O.O.F. Hall (first three-story building in the Gold Country), the remains of the Mayer store, and the beautiful wooden Congregational church, erected in 1856.

The town was started in November, 1848, when hungry miners gave a man named Syree financial backing to open a supply depot for the nearby diggings. In an area ridden by violence and international friction, it seems to have had more than its share. Tradition has it that there was a stretch of 17 weeks when at least one murder was committed every weekend; another "statistic" claims five people were once killed in a single week.

The diggings were rich in this region, so rich that claims were often limited to 16 square feet. But this wealth didn't keep the Americans completely preoccupied. Many other camps had one "racial war," but Mokelumne Hill had two.

South of town, the now-vanished camp of Chili Gulch was the scene of the "Chilean War," a skirmish in which a Chilean claimholder was run out of town by Yankee miners in 1849. The conflict, which claimed several lives, was thought by miners to be justified. It seemed the claimholder had worked his mine with slave labor, even registering claims in the names of men who worked for him. Slavery was one universally forbidden practice in the gold camps.

The "French War," which occurred two years later, was a different matter. French miners who, as a group, had excellent luck in mining, raised their country's flag above their diggings on a hill overlooking the town. Yankees, using the excuse that the French were defying the American government, swarmed up the hill and drove the French from their claims. As far as anyone knows, the excuse was hollow: only envy and greed provoked the incident.

North of town, where State 49 crosses the Mokelumne River, was the site of Big Bar. An important camp in the 1850s, it also had a busy ferry that transported miners, gold, and supplies. When placers gave out, mining activity moved south to the rich diggings in Mokelumne Hill.

North of Big Bar, the badly weathered Ginocchio store, built in 1856 and now protected by a sturdy fence, is the sole survivor of Butte City, a camp that rivaled Jackson until mining ended.

Lodging

Hotel Leger

P.O. Box 50
Mokelumne Hill, CA 95245
209/286-1401 **$$**

Popular saloon, breakfast room, and pool. This handsome (albeit somewhat weathered) hotel was built in 1851. When the county seat was moved to San Andreas in 1866, George W. Leger incorporated the adjoining courthouse building into his hotel. All seven rooms have private baths.

Jackson

Jackson, Amador's county seat, shows a modern face to visitors, but city planners strive to preserve remnants of its Gold Rush period. Most of historic Main Street was rebuilt shortly after being destroyed by fire in 1862. From a hillside overview north of town, Highway 49 drivers get peeks at two of the deepest (over 5,000 feet), richest, and best-known quartz mines in the Mother Lode.

The Argonaut, recognizable today only by its lofty headframe, opened in 1850 and operated off and on for almost a century. In 1922, 47 men were trapped below the surface by fire in the mine. Frantic rescue operations, lasting for three weeks, were conducted through the connecting tunnels of the Kennedy Mine. When the miners were located, all were dead. A carbide lamp had been used to write a grisly finis: "gas too strong—3 A.M."

Jackson started life in 1848 as Bottileas, a label affixed by Mexican and Chilean miners who were impressed by the abundance of bottles dropped at a spring that served as a watering spot for passing miners. A plaque behind the National Hotel, at the foot of Main Street, marks the site of the well.

Another plaque, this one heart shaped, is dedicated with tongue in cheek to the city's "ladies of the evening." In fact, Jackson was the last city in California to have legalized prostitution.

Stop by the Amador County Chamber of Commerce (west side of Highway 49 at the intersection of Highways 49 and 88) to pick up brochures on area attractions. Note particularly the I.O.O.F. Hall (reputedly the country's tallest three-story building), St. Patrick's Catholic Church and the United Methodist Church (both date from the 1860s), and the pink Chichizola Store (beyond the Tailing Wheels on Jackson Gate Road) that dates from the 1850s.

Photo courtesy of Martin Litton

Tailing Wheels, Jackson

Historic Attractions

Amador County Museum

225 Church Street
Jackson
209/223-6386

On a hill overlooking Main Street, the former Brown family residence, built in 1894, houses the county's collection of memorabilia. Many of the furnishings are original. Of special interest is the building housing detailed working models of the Kennedy Mine. *Open 10 A.M. to 4 P.M. Wednesday through Sunday; Kennedy Mine model tour hourly 11 A.M. to 3 P.M. weekends only. Donations; extra $1 for mine tour.*

Kennedy Mine Tailing Wheels

Off Jackson Gate Road, an extension
of North Main Street
Jackson

Walk up well-marked trails to get a close look at the huge tailing wheels erected in 1912 to carry waste gravels up and over the hills into a settling pond. Only two of the original wheels are still standing, one on each side of the road. The others lie in ruins, victims of the elements and age.

St. Sava Serbian Orthodox Church

724 North Main Street
Jackson

This tiny chapel, noted for its unusual architectural style, is the mother church of Serbian Orthodox religion for the entire North American continent. Built in 1894, it recently hosted members from Serbian communities around the world for its centennial.

Chaw'se Indian Grinding Rock State Historic Park

Pine Grove-Volcano Road
Pine Grove, CA 95665
209/296-7488

Excellent museum, re-created village. Pine and oak trees shade a campground with 22 RV or tent sites (reserve through MISTIX,

800/444-7275). This 135-acre park in the pines is named for the huge bedrock mortar that the Miwoks used to grind their food. The 7,700-square-foot limestone outcropping with its 1,158 mortar holes and 363 petroglyph designs is so impressive that a replica was made for the Smithsonian Institution in Washington, D.C.

Before the Gold Rush, Native Americans met here in the fall when the acorns were ripe. Using the rock and with stone pestles as utensils, they ground acorns, berries, and seeds into palatable food. During the Big Days celebrations in late September, Miwoks perform ritual dances, explain their crafts, and offer tastes of Native American food. *Open daily. Modest admission per vehicle.*

Daffodil Hill

Shake Ridge Road
3 miles north of Volcano
209/296-7048

Every spring acres of daffodils carpet the slopes of a pioneer homestead known as the McLaughlin Ranch. Lovingly tended by descendants of the original settlers, the acres of golden blooms are visited by thousands of people annually. *Open only during blooming season, mid-March to early April. Picnic sites. Donations.*

Springtime, Daffodil Hill   Photo courtesy of Larry Angier

Diversions

Gold Panning tours

Roaring Camp Mining Co. *(209/296-4100)*, offers chances to pan for gold during the summer in the deep Mokelumne River canyon. Tours range from half-day jaunts (dinner and music) to week-long stays in fairly primitive cabins.

Water sports

Bring along your fishing pole, bathing suit, water-skiis, and boat on a visit to the Central Mother Lode. On the west side of Highway 49 between San Andreas and Jackson (a distance of some 15 miles), four reservoirs offer a complete range of water sports.

Camanche Lake *(209/763-5166)*, the largest, is on the Mokelumne River. Boating, fishing (bass, bluegill, catfish, crappie, kokanee, sunfish, and trout), swimming, and water-skiing are allowed; boat rentals, cottages, and campsites are available. To reach the south shore, follow State 12 west from San Andreas about 20 miles; the north shore is 15 miles west of Jackson off State 88.

Lake Pardee *(209/772-1472)*, upstream on the Mokelumne, is known for its fishing, particularly kokanee. Swimming and water skiing are not allowed. Facilities include a swimming pool, marina with boat rentals, picnic areas, and campsites. To reach the lake, turn west off State 49 in Jackson onto Hoffman Lane (Stony Creek Road) and continue about 10 miles.

Lake Amador *(209/274-2625)*, on Jackson Creek has about 13 miles of shoreline and a 200-foot-deep main channel. It's large enough to appeal to anglers (bass are big) and its size makes it seem relatively uncrowded. A large pool overlooks the lake, and a coffee shop is located at the entrance. Fees include swimming, fishing, and picnicking (no water-skiing allowed). Boat-launching and camping are extra. From Jackson, take Highway 88 west to Jackson Valley Road, turn south, and follow signs through Buena Vista.

New Hogan Reservoir *(209/772-1343)*, on the Calaveras River is often overlooked by tourists, but it offers fishing, boating, swimming, and water-skiing. There are campgrounds and picnic areas along the shore. To get there, take Highway 12 west from San Andreas to Valley Springs; turn south and follow the signs for about three miles.

Wine Tasting

If you plan a visit to Ione and Buena Vista (see Side Trips below), don't overlook two of the area's wineries. Open Wednesday through Sunday, both **Greenstone Winery** *(Highway 88 at Jackson Valley Road)* and **Jackson Valley Winery** *(4851 Buena Vista Road)* make worthwhile tasting and picnicking sites.

Lodging

The Heirloom

214 Shakeley Lane
P.O. Box 322
Ione, CA 95640
209/274-4468 **$$**

Delightful grounds surround this lovingly decorated Southern antebelllum mansion (built in 1863), which lies just slightly more than a driver's length away from a championship golf course. In the main house, four guest rooms are named for seasons; two "Rooms for All Seasons" are housed in an unusual rammed-earth adobe. Rates include delicious full breakfasts and afternoon snacks.

Court Street Inn

215 Court Street
Jackson, CA 95642
209/223-0416 **$$**

This handy location within strolling distance of downtown offers six rooms and baths, all loaded with antique furnishings. The setting is an 1872 Victorian cottage with garden. Good breakfast, evening appetizers, and a hot tub round out the amenities.

National Hotel

2 Water Street
Jackson, CA 95642
209/223-0500 $

In continuous operation since 1862, this historic hotel has registered Will Rogers, John Wayne, Leland Stanford, and other notables as guests through the years. The 35 upstairs bedrooms (some with private baths) could use refurbishing, but the Old West-type saloon and downstairs gourmet restaurant (Michael's) are crowd-pleasers.

Wedgewood Inn

11941 Narcissus Road
Jackson, CA 95642
209/296-4300 $$

This modern "Victorian" has five individually decorated rooms and a carriage house (all with private baths) set on a wooded site off Highway 88 east of town. Honeymooners will enjoy the seclusion. Rates include a full breakfast.

St. George Hotel

2 Main Street, P.O. Box 9
Volcano, CA 95689
209/296-4458 $

Even if you don't stay here, stop for a drink in the bar. Weekend breakfast or Saturday night dinner in the adjoining dining room is also fun. The three-story hotel has been here since 1862. It's no longer the pride of the Mother Lode, but the 20 rooms (some with private baths) are neat and clean.

Dining

Buscaglia's

1218 Jackson Gate Road
Jackson
209/223-9992 $

This traditional Italian restaurant has been serving guests since 1916. Sunday afternoon chicken dinner is a favorite with locals.

The bar is crowded and the music loud most weekends. *Open for lunch Wednesday through Friday, dinner Wednesday through Sunday. Reservations required weekends.*

Cafe Max Swiss Bakery

140 Main Street
Jackson
209/223-0174 $

The city's favorite bakery recently added a cafe offering sandwiches and other light fare. *Open daily for morning coffee, lunch, and afternoon snacks.*

Teresa's

1235 Jackson Gate Road
Jackson
209/223-1786 $

This well respected Italian restaurant (across from Buscaglia's) has been owned and operated by the same family since 1921. *Open daily for lunch and dinner except Wednesday and Thursday.*

Upstairs

164 Main Street
Jackson
209/223-3342 $

Paintings adorn walls and linens cover tables in this small balconied restaurant overlooking Main Street. The continental-style cuisine is updated with light sauces and fresh herbs. *Open Tuesday through Sunday for lunch and dinner.*

Giannini's

Highway 88
Pine Grove
209/296-7222 $

Third-generation restaurant owners serve a variety of Northern Italian specialties in the town's most historic building. The small Canopy Room's comfortable booths make it the best place to sit. *Open Thursday through Sunday for dinner. Reservations suggested on Friday and Saturday.*

Side Trips

Volcano

Northeast of Jackson off Highway 88 lies Volcano. This is unquestionably one of the most interesting stops in the Gold Country—not only for what it was in the 1850s but for what it is today. Volcano's earliest residents were a lively bunch, as intent on developing their little city as they were for digging gold. Today's residents are equally lively and intent on preserving its heritage.

The town's name is a misnomer. Though it is located in a natural cup in the mountains, there is nothing volcanic about the area's mountain structure. Evidently, the settlers just took a casual look around them and settled for first impressions.

Gold was first discovered here in 1848 by members of the New York 8th Regiment, Mexican War Volunteers. The first mining camp grew quickly into a city of 5,000 people, and was the lively center of a rich mining area that produced some $90 million in gold. When the placer workings gave out, hydraulic mining tore the soil away from the limestone bedrock and sent it funneling through sluices.

Volcano claims many "firsts" in California's cultural development: first public library, first literary and debating society, first astronomical observatory, first "little theater" movement. It also provided an abundance of saloons and fandango halls to fill the miners' idle hours. At one time there were three dozen saloons and three breweries. One of the carefully marked stone facades standing on the west side of the main street housed two separately operated bars.

There are many other reminders of the early town: an old jail, a brewery built in 1856, the Lavezzo building that once served as a wine shop, and others. All are marked for easy identification. Perhaps the most unusual remnant of Volcano's past is Old Abe, the cannon that helped to win the Civil War without ever firing a shot.

Volcano's Union volunteers wheeled out Old Abe to put down a threatened Confederate uprising. Control of Volcano might have meant that the area's gold would be diverted to aid the Southern cause. The story is told that in the absence of iron cannon balls, Union supporters gathered round, river-smoothed stones. Fortunately, Old Abe won the battle without firing a shot: its mere presence squelched the uprising.

During the 1850s, Volcano and Jackson had a sporting rivalry typical of the era. A Jackson paper once reported that one of its residents caused quite a stir in Volcano when he produced a ten dollar gold piece to pay his hotel bill and buy the house a round of drinks. The editor implied that it had been so long since anyone in Volcano had seen a ten dollar gold piece that they gathered around the Jacksonian with great curiosity and admiration.

It only took a week for the Volcano paper to straighten Jackson around. It wasn't curiosity or admiration of the gold piece, it seems. It was Volcano's awe that anyone from Jackson should have that much cash in the first place, and further that he would use it to buy someone else a drink and to also pay his hotel bill before slipping out of town.

Just south of town, on the Volcano-Pine Grove Road, are limestone caves where the area's first Masons held their meetings. The caverns are a cool oasis during summer heat, but posted warnings indicate they are equally popular with rattlers.

Buena Vista and Ione

Nine miles west of Jackson, at the intersection of the Ione-Buena Vista Road and Jackson Valley Road (off Highway 88), a few buildings mark the site of the old settlement of Buena Vista. An interesting story is told about the old stone building (now a saloon with an adjoining restaurant).

The structure was originally a store built in Lancha Plana, six miles away, by a William Cook. When the miners moved on to richer fields, Chinese miners arrived to scavenge through the tailings, but the only virgin ground was under the store. Cook wanted to move his business to thriving Buena Vista and the Chinese craved the land, so a unique bargain was struck. If they would move the store and rebuild it in Buena Vista, they could have the land gratis. Within several weeks, the building was taken down, stone by stone, and rebuilt at the crossroads where it has been standing for over a century. It's not really known if the land was worth the back-breaking effort.

Ione, north of the junction of Highways 88 and 104, has been around since the earliest days of the Gold Rush, not as a mining camp but as a stage stop, agricultural and rail center, and clay and stone producer. The Dosch Pit, worked since 1864, is the oldest continuously active clay mine in the state.

Like so many other towns that started as temporary camps, Ione's dignified name (she was the heroine of The Last Days of Pompeii) was chosen only after townsfolk grew embarrassed about its two previous names, Freezeout and Bedbug. The Methodist church, built in 1866, is one of the few old buildings still scattered around town.

Today Ione is best known as the location of Mule Creek State Prison, the Preston School of Industry, and the championship Castle Oaks Golf Course. The brooding building on top of the hill is the now-abandoned Preston School of Industry, established in 1889.

Nothing remains of several lively gold camps north of the city except for tales of rich strikes. The colorful tailings and delapidated buildings you notice off Highway 88 between Ione and Jackson are all that remains of the Newton Copper Mine.

Sutter Creek

The self-proclaimed "Nicest Little Town in the Mother Lode" has a lot of visitor appeal. Antique shops, boutiques, restaurants, and bed-and-breakfast inns are housed in venerable buildings along Main Street. Among the most historic structures are the Masonic and I.O.O.F. halls (1865), Methodist church (1862), Malatesta building (1860), iron-shuttered, stone Brignole building (1859), and Bellotti Inn (1860), which was originally the American Exchange Hotel. All are clearly marked on a walking tour map, available at the Bubble Gum Book Store or from other merchants along the route.

Charming New England-style residences are found at the south end of town and along its quiet side streets. The former grammar school off Broad Street, currently home to the Amador County Arts Council, was started in 1870. Sutter Creek's museum is housed in the former Monteverde grocery store on Randolph Street.

Sutter Creek was named for Captain John Sutter, the man who owned the sawmill where gold was first discovered. He camped near here in 1848 with a group of Native Americans. Sutter wasn't looking for gold, only timber. The actual camp got its start when a few early miners erected a community tent to use on rainy Sundays when they couldn't get to Jackson or Drytown.

Sutter Creek achieved permanency as an important supply center for the quartz mines ringing the town. Hetty Green, at one time the richest women in the world due to her financial acumen on Wall Street, once owned the Old Eureka Mine on the south side of town. Tailings are all that remain today.

One of Sutter Creek's most famous success stories concerns Leland Stanford. As a young man, Stanford acquired some wealth as a merchant in Sacramento. He picked up a stake in Sutter Creek's Lincoln Mine as payment of a merchant's debt. He worked the claim but suffered repeated failures. Discouraged, Stanford decided to sell the property for $5,000 but was talked out of it at the last minute by Robert Downs, the mine foreman. Not long after, a big strike was made and the Lincoln (Union) Mine became a bonanza.

With this money as a start, Stanford became a railroad king, a U. S. Senator, Governor of California, and founder of Stanford University. The home of the former Lincoln Mine foreman is located on Spanish Street, across from the Immaculate Conception Catholic church. The mine site is at the north end of town.

Photo courtesy of the Knight Foundry

Historic photo of Knight Foundry in Sutter Creek

Historic Attractions

Knight Foundry

81 Eureka Street, Sutter Creek
209/267-5543

Knight is the last water-powered foundry and machine shop in the world. In continuous operation since 1873 when quartz mining started in the Mother Lode, the foundry designed and manufactured water wheels and other machinery for stamp mills in California, Nevada, Arizona, and Utah. The foundry's own machinery is still quietly run by its original 42-inch water wheel.

Now designated an historical landmark, the foundry continues to produce iron castings for commercial and residential use. In addition to taking a look at foundry operations (call for dates of dramatic "pours" of molten metal, usually one Saturday a month), visitors can watch artisans at work nearby. *Self-guided tours 9 A.M. to 4 P.M. daily except major holidays. Admission $2.50 adults, $1.50 children 6 to 18. Gift shop. Workshops offered several times a year.*

Chew Kee Store

Main Street, Fiddletown

This old rammed-earth adobe served as a model for a reconstruction in Coloma's state park. Built in 1850 with walls over two feet thick, it was originally a Chinese herb shop, then the home of Fiddletown's last Chinese resident, Jimmy Chow, who died in 1965. It still contains many original furnishings and paraphernalia. *Open Saturday noon to 4 P.M. April through October.*

Shenandoah Valley Museum

Sobon Estate winery
14430 Shenandoah Road
Plymouth
209/245-6554

Amador County's wine industry dates back to the days of the Gold Rush. You can get a look at its beginnings in this small but well-designed paean to the past. The free museum is housed in one of the original D'Agostini Winery buildings, which date from 1856.

BONANZA OF SHOPS

Amador City, Sutter Creek, and Jackson are only two miles from each other, making shopping a pleasure. Even tiny Volcano (eight miles east) offers three or four chances to buy that special gift. The town's Little Shamrock Lapidary shop stocks a wealth of crystalline minerals fashioned into windchimes, book ends, and other attractive items, as well as vials of precious gold dust.

Stores with picturesque names are packed with interesting items: the Squirrel's Nest, On Purpose, and Lizzie Ann's in Sutter Creek; Not Just Llamas in Jackson; and the Victorian Closet in Amador City.

Three talented local designers stock boutiques with their own creations. Check out The Goldiggers in Jackson (39 Main Street) for casual attire. In Sutter Creek, Coming Attractions (79 Main Street) features cotton clothing and woven attire, and the Sutter Creek Clothing Co. (32 Main Street) showcases one-of-a-kind hats.

Almost every third store is an antique shop. Some of the best include The Columbian Lady, Water Street Antiques, Sutter Creek Antiques, and Arnold Antiques in Sutter Creek and Sherrill's Country Store in Amador City.

For locally produced fine art and crafts, try the Fine Eye Gallery and Cobweb Collection in Sutter Creek and the Left Bank Gallery and Funk's Pottery Gallery in Jackson. Cooks won't want to miss Jackson's Kitchen Shop, at the intersection of Highway 49 and Main Street.

In Trims and Treasures Christmas Year Round (33 Main Street, Jackson) you'll find egg ornaments painted with Mother Lode scenes. If your ancestors came from Scotland, Amador City's Heather in the Hills shop stocks books that help trace your roots and tartans from all clans.

When shopping palls, try Caffee Tazza (214 Main Street, Jackson), Sutter Creek Coffee Roasting Co. (20 Eureka Street), or Somewhere in Time tea room (34 Main Street, Sutter Creek) for a pick-me-up.

Diversions

Claypipers

Piper Playhouse
Highway 49
Drytown
209/245-4604

Founded by a theatrical troupe from the San Francisco Bay Area in 1957, the Claypipers are the oldest continuously running melodramatic group in the state. Show-goers hiss the villain, cheer the hero, and sigh for the poor heroine in old-fashioned performances where virtue always triumphs. Between-scenes song and dance numbers are crowd-pleasers. *Melodrama offered at 8 P.M. Saturday nights from Memorial Day weekend through September. Reservations suggested.*

Wine touring

Shenandoah Valley, east of Plymouth

Pack a picnic lunch before you enter Amador's answer to the Napa Valley. More than a dozen small wineries, most with tasting rooms and picnic sites, cluster on or around Shenandoah Road. Some award winners include state-of-the-art Amador Foothill Winery, Montevina Winery (dramatic building), Karly Winery (basket collection), Renwood-Santino Winery (large gift shop), Shenandoah Vineyards (art displays/wine recipe book), Sobon Estate (museum), Spinetta Vineyards (imposing wildlife art gallery), and Story Winery (grand canyon views). *Most wineries open daily from spring through fall, weekends the rest of the year.*

Lodging

Sutter Creek Inn

75 Main Street
P.O. Box 385
Sutter Creek, CA 95685
209/267-5606 **$$**

Built around 1859, this gracious house was once the residence of California Senator E.C. Voorhies. In the 1960s, innkeeper Jane

Way turned it into the first inn west of the Mississippi. The main house and outbuildings scattered around extensive gardens contain 18 large air-conditioned rooms, many with fireplaces, sitting areas, private patios, and swinging beds (they can be stabilized). Rates include family-style breakfasts. Appointments needed for massage or handwriting analysis. Games and books fill the spacious living room.

Sutter Creek Inn　　　　　Photo courtesy of Sutter Creek Inn

The Foxes

77 Main Street
P.O. Box 159
Sutter Creek, CA 95685
209/267-5882 **$$$**

A tailored garden, made-to-order breakfasts, and an impeccable decor make this seven-room inn a popular choice. Once known as the Brinn House, the 1850s residence has been renovated and refurbished by the owners.

Grey Gables Inn

161 Hanford Street
P.O.Box 1687
Sutter Creek, CA 95685
209/267-1039 **$$**

Britain comes to the Mother Lode with English owners, gardens, and eight rooms named for that country's poets. All the nicely decorated rooms have baths and fireplaces. Breakfast, tea, and evening refreshments are included in the rates.

Imperial Hotel

14202 Highway 49
Amador City, CA 95601
209/267-9172 **$$**

A restored, century-old brick hotel is home to an acclaimed restaurant and bar and six delightful, whimsically decorated bedrooms. Though its balcony overlooks Main Street, Room 1 is most popular. Breakfast comes to you or is served in the dining room.

Mine House

14125 Highway 49
Amador City, CA 95601
209/267-5900 **$$**

Formerly the Keystone Mine office, this recently updated inn has eight rooms and baths, all but one named for their original use—Vault, Retort, Assay, Stores, Grinding, Directors, Bookkeeping, and Keystone. A large continental breakfast is brought to your room. A swimming pool cools you off on hot summer days.

Old Well Motel

Highway 49
Drytown, CA 95699
209/245-6467 **$**

A nicely kept lawn and pool front these air-conditioned cabins, which are Drytown's only public lodging. Next door is the Old Well Grill, a local favorite, and across the street is the Claypipers theater.

Shenandoah Inn

17674 Village Drive
Plymouth, CA 95669
209/245-3888 $

At the south end of town, this two-story Best Western has 47 comfortable rooms, most offering views of the rolling grasslands, and a pool. The Bar-T-Bar Restaurant is just up the street.

Dining

Buffalo Chips Emporium

Highway 49
Amador City
209/267-0570 $

Locals and tourists alike enjoy a light meal in this attractively decorated diner. Don't leave without trying one of Maria's mouth-watering pies (rhubarb is a favorite) or a milkshake from the old-fashioned soda fountain. *Open Wednesday through Sunday 9 A.M. to 5 P.M.*

Imperial Hotel Restaurant

14202 Highway 49
Amador City
209/267-9172 $$

Decor and cuisine are both creatively designed and presented in this dining room, the area's favorite. Don't overlook the garlic and Brie appetizer, and save room for dessert. *Open daily 5 P.M. to 9 P.M. for dinner, Sunday brunch 10 A.M. to 2 P.M. Full bar. Reservations required on weekends.*

Sutter Creek Palace

76 Main Street
Sutter Creek
209/267-1355 $

Sometimes referred to as the "Cheers" of Sutter Creek, the Palace serves a variety of dishes. A favorite menu item is the popular prime rib. *Bar with music on the weekends.*

Side Trips

North to Amador City, Drytown, and Plymouth

Tucked snugly into a fold of the foothills, Amador City is two miles north of Sutter Creek and is bisected by Highway 49. Its block-long Main Street has a lot to offer travelers: a multitude of quaint shops, good restaurants, and renovated historic hotels. Though the Amador Hotel's former rooms have been replaced by small shops, the Imperial Hotel still accepts guests (see Lodging above). Note also the little hillside cemetery.

Jose Maria Amador, a ranchero from what is now the San Ramon Valley, gave his name to the little town and the county that was separated from Calaveras County in 1854. The first quartz discovery in the county was made here by a Baptist preacher. Because of his association with several other men of the cloth, the strike was known as the Ministers' Claim.

Quartz mining provided the economic base for Amador City, and the headframe of the very rich Keystone Mine can be seen on the eastern slope above the south side of town. The Mine House (see "Lodging" above) is located in the original mine headquarters.

A pleasant country lane, paralleling Highway 49 between Amador City and Drytown (two miles to the north), passes through the sites of the Bunker Hill, New Philadelphia, and New Chicago mines. Little of historic interest remains except for a few foundations and remnants of stone fences.

Founded in 1848, Drytown is Amador County's oldest community. From its name you might guess that it had been settled by men of abstemious habit. But the town actually supported 26 saloons in its prime, and temperance was not a widespread virtue. Dry Creek was the source of the moniker.

The placer diggings gave out in 1857, and a fire soon leveled the town. However, several brick buildings, dating from 1851, still attest to the boom. Near the corner of the Claypipers Theatre, a road to the east leads past an adobe and rock house. Though its exact age is unknown, the residence was referred to as an "old adobe in Drytown" in an 1856 history of the area.

A legend lingers that $80,000 in gold bullion is buried somewhere under the Old Well Motel's swimming pool. It seems that during the Gold Rush a posse was waiting when bandits staged a payroll holdup. After a chase to the basement of a storehouse that stood on this site, the outlaws were killed, but supposedly they had already buried the gold.

Incidentally, there is no public access to the old cemetery on the hill guarded by cypresses. Interesting tombstones date back to the early 1850s.

Two miles east of Drytown, on a back road between Drytown and Amador City, is the site of Lower Rancheria—a predominantly Mexican and Chilean mining camp dating back to 1848. A series of robberies and murders were perpetrated here on the night of August 6, 1855, by a gang of 12 Mexican horsemen. As a result of the tragedy, Yankeee miners arose en masse and demanded that every Mexican be disarmed and driven from the region. Tempers eventually cooled, but not until much injustice had been done.

A monument marking the mass grave of the Dyman family, killed in the massacre, can be reached by a side road from Amador City. It is on a hill to the right of Rancheria Creek, about a quarter-mile from the road.

During the 1850s, the settlements of Plymouth and Pokerville grew up side by side on a dry flat. Plymouth is now the gateway to the Shenandoah Valley vineyards east of town and the location of Amador County's fairgrounds; Pokerville has all but vanished. The headframe and tailings from the Plymouth Consolidated Mines, which produced over $13 million in gold, are still evident. The most notable structure in town, the Empire building on Main Street, was the mining company's brick office.

Nashville to the north, originally called Quartzburg, was one of the state's earliest quartz-mining districts. The first stamp mill in the Mother Lode was made in Cincinnati and brought around the Horn from the East Coast to be installed at the Tennessee Mine. Traces of headframes and a mining dump can still be seen.

Fiddletown

About six miles east from Highway 49 at Plymouth lies Fiddletown. This sleepy, tree-shaded village lies in the center of a prosperous dry farming belt that is still worked in some cases by descendants of the pioneers who settled here in the 1850s. During the Gold Rush, Fiddletown was a sprawling collection of shacks and miners' tents and boasted the largest Chinese settlement in California outside of San Francisco.

The flavor of those early days is preserved by a few old structures, all within a couple of blocks. The building across from the herbal doctor's home and office (see Historic Attractions) was once a Chinese gambling house. Up the street is The Forge, originally a blacksmith shop built around 1852. One of the best-preserved structures is the Shallhorne Blacksmith and Wagon Shop, built circa 1870.

Fiddletown's fame must, in part, rest on its name. Founded by Missourians in 1849, it was named by an elder in the group who described the younger men as "always fiddling." It kept the name until 1878 when it was changed to Oleta at the insistence of a Judge Purinton, who was embarrassed to be known in Sacramento and San Francisco as that "man from Fiddletown." The old name, whose charm was quickly recognized by Bret Harte and immortalized by him in An Episode in Fiddletown, was restored in the 1920s.

It was here that a certain Judge Yates reached the limit of his patience in listening to an outlandish whopper and created a classic in courtroom procedure. After hearing all he could stand, he finally turned to the witness, banged down the gavel, and said, "I declare court adjourned. This man is a damned liar." After this statement, he again banged his gavel and stated, "Court in session."

The Wells Fargo Company once had $10,000 stolen from their safe in Fiddletown. A mob quickly assembled to hang the supposedly guilty party. They strung their man up several times but sympathizers kept cutting him down. He protested his innocence and finally the deputy sheriff and a doctor arrived on the scene. They cut him down and revived him, but he was paralyzed for months. It was later discovered that their victim had not even been in town the night of the robbery, and that one of the members of the hanging mob was the actual culprit.

Placerville

In the 1850s, Placerville was the second largest town in the Mother Lode. First settled in 1848 by miners who branched out from Coloma, the camp was a supply center, a stopping place for goldseekers on their way north and south, and a station on the Pony Express route. Today, it's a stop for motorists on busy U.S. Highway 50 between Sacramento and Lake Tahoe.

Called Dry Diggin's because of the scarcity of water to wash its gold-laden soils, it became one of the most prosperous camps in the Mother Lode. Three prospectors—Daylor, Sheldon, and McCoon—made the first strike, taking $17,000 in gold in one week.

The settlement's name was changed to Hangtown in 1849 after a series of grisly lynchings, and finally to Placerville in 1854 to satisfy local pride. But Hangtown was not a misnomer. There are several on record, the first of which was actually a triple hanging. Two Mexicans and a Yankee were accused of robbing a Frenchman named Caillous of 50 ounces of gold dust and were strung up after only a single night's deliberation. "Irish Dick" Crone was another who felt the hangman's noose after he knifed a man to death over a turn of the cards in a gambling game. Two Frenchmen and a Chilean were set swinging for a crime that no one can seem to remember.

When the Comstock Lode was discovered in Nevada, the road east from Placerville became the main route across the mountains for miners eager to abandon the fading gold fields for the promise of silver. Mark Twain tells a humorous story of Horace Greeley's jolting ride over the road with Hank Monk (one of the most famous of the stage drivers) in Roughing It. Supposedly Monk said "Keep your seat, Horace, and I'll get you there on time!" Twain goes on to add "and you bet he did, too, what was left of him!"

Placerville attracted many colorful characters, some of whom went on to become rich and famous. Three well-known citizens were Phillip Armour, who ran a butcher shop, and Mark Hopkins and Collis Huntington, who were grocers in the town's Gold Rush days and later became railroad tycoons. Another was J. M. Studebaker, a wheelwright who stuck to his trade instead of mining. From 1853 to 1858 Studebaker made wheelbarrows for the miners at his shop at 543 Main Street (a plaque marks the location). With about $8,000 in savings he returned to South Bend, Indiana, and he and his brothers built what became the largest pioneer wagon factory in the world. This same factory later served as the foundation for the Studebaker Corporation.

Though Placerville has long since outgrown its historic center at the bottom of the ravine, its street pattern is still based on the trails marked off by the miners' pack mules. Poet Edwin Markham is among early pioneers buried at the Placerville City Cemetery on Chamberlain Street.

In the main business district a few old buildings still survive. A Pony Express historical marker can be found in an alley behind a building on Sacramento Street that was a harness shop when built in 1858. The brick and stone City Hall was built in 1860 as a firehouse. The building next door dates from 1862 and was built from funds accumulated by Immigrant Jane Stuart, who sold a herd of horses she had driven across the plains to set up a bawdy house. A single-story rock building on the south side of Main Street, erected in 1852, was one of the few structures to withstand the great fire of 1856 that destroyed almost all of old Hangtown. The I.O.O.F. Hall has been in use since 1859.

The three-story Cary House at 300 Main Street, housing a hotel and shops, takes its name from one of two older hotels that stood on this site. Mark Twain once lodged at the original Cary House (erected after the Raffles Hotel burned in 1856) and, in 1859, Horace Greeley delivered an address to the miners from here. Nearby, The site of the original hangman's tree is marked by a dangling dummy. The bell that called out vigilantes (and volunteer firemen) hangs in a plaza at the intersection of Main and Center streets.

HANGTOWN FRY

First whipped up in Placerville (known as Hangtown in Gold Rush days), this one-skillet egg and oyster dish was created to satisfy the tastes of a miner who struck it rich. Since eggs sold for around 50 cents each and bacon and oysters were worth more than gold, such a meal cost $6 to $7, a fortune in those days. This historic meal might have been called the first "California cuisine."

The following recipe from the Zinfandel Cookbook (Toyon Hill Press, Palo Alto, CA 94306; 800/600-9086) is a little more sophisticated rendition of that early meal.

2 large eggs
1 tablespoon milk
1/4 teaspoon salt
Dash of pepper
1/8 teaspoon ground nutmeg
1/3 cup oysters
All-purpose flour
1 tablespoon butter
1 tablespoon chopped parsley
3 strips crisply fried bacon or browned link sausages

Break eggs into a small bowl and add milk, salt, pepper, and nutmeg. Beat with a fork just enough to mix yolks and whites.

Cut oysters in half, if large; leave small ones whole. Dust oysters with flour. Melt butter in a 7- to 8-inch nonstick frying pan over medium-high heat. Add oysters and cook for 30 seconds on each side.

Pour egg mixture into pan. As eggs begin to set around edges, lift edges and let uncooked egg flow underneath. When eggs no longer flow freely, run a spatula around edge of omelet and flip onto a plate, bottom side up. Sprinkle with parsley and garnish with bacon or sausages.

Makes 1 serving.

Historic Attractions

Gold Bug Mine

Gold Bug Park
N. Bedford Avenue, one mile north
of downtown Placerville
916/642-5232

Touring the illuminated shaft of the nation's only city-owned mine and visiting the stamp mill on the hill above gives visitors a good look at how hardrock mining was done. Even the gold vein is still apparent. Only the feverish activity that once took place here is missing. *Open daily May through September (weekends only spring and fall) for self-guided tours ($1 adults, half-price seniors and children 6 to 16); audio tape and recorder rental $1. Guided tours weekdays ($25) with a week's advance notice. Picnic sites and hiking trails.*

Photo courtesy of the City of Placerville

Placerville's Gold Bug Mine in Bedford Park

El Dorado County Historical Museum

100 Placerville Drive
El Dorado County Fairgrounds
Placerville
916/621-5865

This large museum offers a good look at the area's golden past, with special emphasis on equipment and vehicles, from Studebaker's wheelbarrow and Snowshoe Thompson's skis to a stagecoach and Shay locomotive. *Open 10 A.M. to 4 P.M. Wednesday through Saturday year-round, plus Sunday afternoons from March through October. Donations.*

Fountain-Tallman City Museum

524 Main Street
Placerville

Mementos and memorabilia of the city's past are housed in what was once a soda water works. In addition to a machine that makes soda water, the museum also features a room of Victorian furniture that once belonged to San Francisco millionaire William Ralston. *Open weekend afternoons. Donations.*

Diversions

Apple Hill

Take U.S. 50 east of Placerville to the
Camino turnoff a few miles down the road

The hills east of Placerville are covered with apple trees. In autumn, when trees are heavy with fruit, the farms and orchards of this upcountry are alive with visitors who come to pick the crunchy fruit, sample apple butter and apple pies, and buy gifts.

Almost a dozen small wineries throughout the region (most in Somerset) also welcome guests. The oldest, Boeger Winery (1709 Carson Road, Placerville; tasting room open daily) dates back to 1870.

Lodging

Camellack-Blair House

3059 Cedar Ravine
Placerville, CA 95667
916/622-3764 $$

You can't miss this ornate pink Queen Anne Victorian. From the wicker-furnished front verandah to the swing on the back porch, it's a turn-of-the-century period piece complete with spiral staircase. Antique furniture and lots of lace adorn the three guest rooms (two with private baths). Breakfast is included in the rate.

Chichester-McKee House

800 Spring Street
Placerville, CA 95667
916/626-1882 $$

Built in 1892, this Victorian residence was Placerville's finest — and the first to boast indoor plumbing. Today, updated and refurbished, it still has that touch of elegance despite a busy Highway 49 location. All three rooms have fireplaces and half-baths.

Placerville Inn

U.S. 50 at Missouri Flat Road
Placerville, CA
916/622-9100 $

Situated in the middle of apple and wine country, this 105-room modern motel offers travelers a heated pool and jacuzzi. Brawley's Restaurant, located nearby, is open all day.

American River Inn

Corner of Main and Orleans Street, P.O. Box 43
Georgetown, CA 95634
800/245-6566 $$

In the days of the Gold Rush, this survivor was a miners' boarding house called the American Hotel. Today it's a stylish and very comfortable inn complete with pool and spa, putting green, driving range, and croquet lawn. Rates for the lovingly decorated 25 rooms include breakfast.

Dining

Smith Flat House
2021 Smith Flat Road
1 mile east of Placerville off U.S. 50
at Point View Road exit
916/621-0667 $

Though this historic restaurant has been around for a while, the building is much older. Among its previous incarnations, the 1850s structure has been a stage stop, dance hall, store, and hotel. You'll feel just like a prospector in the old-fashioned basement bar, which is carved out of rock. *Open for lunch Monday through Saturday, dinner Tuesday through Sunday.*

Lil' Mama D. Carlo's
482 Main Street
Placerville
916/626-1612 $

As the name would indicate, this established restaurant in the heart of downtown serves hearty Italian cuisine. *Open for lunch weekdays, dinner daily.*

Side trips

Southern loop

Not much remains of historical interest south of Placerville, but the small towns south of U.S. Highway 50 were all thriving camps during the Gold Rush.

Diamond Springs was a stop on the Carson Emigrant Trail and one of the richest spots in the area, with a population of 1,500. Now, with gold gone and traffic rerouted, the old part of town dozes in the sun. Antique shops fill the vintage Louis LePetit Store, and the grand old frame I.O.O.F. Hall, built in 1852 on a foundation of brick and dressed stone, stands on a hill north of the main street.

Only a few stone relics still stand in El Dorado, which was known as Mud Springs when it was the center of rich placer diggings. The town had been a stop on the Carson Emigrant Trail, but was not named until the miners arrived in 1849 and 1850. The Wells Fargo Express office is now Poor Red's (lunch weekdays, dinner nightly), a cafe whose barbecued ribs attract travelers from as far away as Sacramento. Murals on the bar's walls depict the main street as it appeared in the 1850s.

Shingle Springs to the east was named for a cool spring that flowed near a shingle mill built before mining started in 1850. A marker on a fine old native stone building at the west end of town designates it as the original shingle mill, although there is considerable disagreement over this claim.

Georgetown

The 28-mile loop trip to Georgetown on Highway 193 is worth the drive simply for the views you receive as the road twists, turns, and dips into the canyon of the South Fork of the American River at Chili Bar, a favorite put-in spot for rafters. In the early days, many of the Chileans working at the rich gold bar in the river were killed by a smallpox epidemic. Bodies, at first buried on the bar, were later moved to higher ground. A stone plaque marks the site.

The highway passes through Kelsey, where James Marshall had a blacksmith shop after giving up hope of striking it rich. Little else remains to suggest that this was once one of the rowdiest of the gold camps, with six hotels and 24 saloons.

Photogenic Georgetown is a hidden surprise, particularly if you make the trip in spring when spectacular displays of wild Scotch broom cover the hillsides. The mining camp got its start in 1849 when George Phipps and a party of sailors struck it rich while working the stream below the present townsite.

The camp was first named Growlersburg because the gravels were so rich the nuggets "growled" in the miners' pans. Tents were the most popular form of architecture until a photographer, taking a "flash" picture of a dead miner in a gambling hall, started a fire that leveled the entire town in 1852. When it was rebuilt, it was laid out with the inordinately wide streets you see today. (The main street is a full 100 feet across; side streets are 60 feet wide.)

WHITE-WATER BOATING

When the Sierra snowpack turns to water, the Sierra Nevada foothills are favorite thoroughfares for kayakers, canoers, and rafters. Depending on the amount of snow, California's boating season runs from late spring through summer.

River runs are ranked according to speed, water volume, and obstacles. The levels increase in difficulty from Class I to Class VI, the latter usually considered too dangerous to run. To get a list of river outfitters, call the California Outdoor Hotline at (800) 552-3625.

Most outfitters recommend novices start with a Class II or Class III trip, which guarantees you'll get wet but not scared. The scenic North Fork of the American River and the Merced River are suitable for first-time paddlers.

One of the best Class III trips is down the South Fork of the American River through some of the state's most beautiful canyons. One-day runs start at Coloma State Park and end at Folsom Lake; half-day and longer trips are also available. Class III trips should also be possible on the Stanislaus River.

For thrill seekers looking for Class IV and V rafting, the wild and scenic Tuolumne River might be a good bet.

By 1855, there were 3,000 people enjoying the cultural life that included events at a town hall and theater, and Georgetown was referred to as the "Pride of the Mountains."

Much of that character is preserved today with buildings from the 1850s standing alongside country houses added much later.

A two-story wooden survivor, the Georgetown Hotel was built on the site of the Nevada House, an even earlier hostelry. The Shannon Knox House, Georgetown's oldest residence, was constructed with lumber shipped around the Horn. The Balsar House, a former three-story hotel and dance hall built in 1859, became the town's Opera House in 1870 and the I.O.O.F. Hall in 1889 when the top floor was removed. The brick Old Armory (1862) originally had no windows.

Greenwood, west of Georgetown on Highway 193, began in 1848 when trapper John Greenwood and his two sons set up a store to provide supplies to the hungry miners. The town grew to a respectable size in the early years and boasted among other things a well-attended theater. Gold Rush song writer, John A. Stone, known as "Old Putt," is buried in the Pioneer Cemetery under a stone slab marked "J.A.S." and dated January 24, 1863.

The Georgetown Road (Highway 193) rejoins Highway 49 at Cool, a former stage stop on the Auburn-Georgetown Road. When you leave Cool, the road descends about 1,000 feet into the American River Canyon. A few thousand feet upstream soars the Foresthill Bridge, built to cross water that would be impounded if the Auburn Dam is completed. The dam would deepen and widen the Middle and North Forks of the American River for some 25 miles.

Photo courtesy of Martin Litton

I.O.O.F. Hall in Georgetown, Eldorado County

JAMES MARSHALL—
THE MAN WHO STARTED IT ALL

The saddest figure of California's Gold Rush has to be James Wilson Marshall. Despite the fact that he was the first to discover gold, Marshall never made any money from his discovery, and his fame only led to a life of misery. His gold discovery was an accident. If he had not picked up those few flakes of gold at Sutter's mill, then someone else would have found it somewhere else within a year or so. There was just too much gold on the surface to be ignored.

James Marshall was born in New Jersey in 1810, given a moderate education for the day, and taught his father's trade as a millwright. Like many young men of his time, young James started west seeking fame and fortune, arriving at Sutter's Fort in July, 1845, about 10 years after leaving New Jersey.

In August, 1847, Sutter and Marshall agreed to build a sawmill in the foothills, with Sutter to provide the men and money and Marshall the leadership. It was when this mill was almost completed that Marshall found gold in the tailrace on January 24, 1848.

After the discovery, Marshall and Sutter tried to claim ownership of the Coloma property and charge a commission for any gold found by other miners; only a few of the most gullible newcomers paid. Marshall's continued haggling got the miners so riled up that they finally attacked the mill-hands and drove Marshall off the land.

It was at this point that Marshall seriously undermined his own future. He began to claim supernatural power that enabled him to pinpoint the richest gold deposits. When he refused to divulge the location of any of these rich diggings, the miners grew very resentful and even threatened to lynch Marshall if he didn't lead them to the treasure.

Marshall fled for his life, and tried to start over as just another miner. But his face was too well known, and greedy miners dogged his every step in the vain hope that a new bonanza would be uncovered on Marshall's next claim. This constant harrassment turned him into a bitter man, who felt that the world, or at least the state, owed him something for his sensational discovery. He became a recluse, and his eccentric behavior turned away all but a few close friends.

After the state appropriated the discoverer of gold a $200-a-month pension in 1872, Marshall moved to Kelsey, lived in the Union Hotel, and built a blacksmith shop. He remained there until his death in August 1885, at the age of 73. The state pension had been cut in half after 1874 and eliminated in 1876, forcing Marshall to spend his last years doing handyman jobs, seeking handouts, and picking up a few pennies by selling his autograph.

Margaret A. Kelley, a friend of Marshall's during his embittered old age, once wrote that "probably no man ever went to his grave so misunderstood, so misjudged, so misrepresented, so altogether slandered as James W. Marshall." This may be true, but it is also true that Marshall made the worst of his fate. Instead of building on his good fortune, he misplayed it into the instrument of his destruction.

Coloma

This is where it all began. On a cold January morning in 1848, James Marshall, foreman at John Sutter's sawmill, picked up a few flakes of gold in the millrace and started the Gold Rush that changed the history of a nation and the economy of a whole planet.

By summer of 1848, there were 2,000 miners living on the banks of the river: the settlement's population swelled to 10,000 by the next year. Virtually all of the prospectors in the foothills started placer mining at Coloma before branching out to newer strikes. It was here, too, that Gold Rush inflation hit the hardest: picks and shovels sold for $50 each, and foodstuffs went for astronomical prices.

Though Coloma was the first boom town in the foothills, it wasn't long lived. By 1852, there wasn't much of the shiny metal left, and a good part of the population moved on to more golden pastures.

Coloma was the scene of one of the Gold Country's most celebrated double hangings in 1855. One of the principals was Mickey Free, a robber and murderer. The other was Dr. Crane, a teacher convicted of murdering a young lady named Susan who had been foolish enough to reject his proposal of marriage.

The town made quite an affair of the proceedings, even hiring a brass band from Placerville. The crowd was in a holiday mood, and even the doomed men appeared to enter into the spirit of the occasion. With the noose around his neck, Dr. Crane sang several verses of a song he had composed as his departing message, and topped off the performance with "Here I come, Susan!" as the trap fell. Mickey Free, not to be outdone, rounded out the show with an improvised jig, and then unwittingly climaxed the day by writhing to his death by strangulation after the noose slipped and failed to snap his neck. Visitors can still find Free's final resting place at the edge of the Coloma cemetery.

THE FORTUNES OF
JOHN SUTTER

The discovery of gold at his sawmill in Coloma offered John Sutter a golden opportunity to become one of the greatest men in California history. Instead, it ruined him. By 1852, he had lost all of the land and prestige that had taken years to develop, and he had to leave California a bankrupt and broken man.

In many ways, Sutter was one of the most appealing of the California pioneers, and his settling of the Sacramento Valley was one of the most important milestones in the state's history. On the other hand, many aspects of his personal life are appalling, and most of his problems were the direct result of his own irresponsibility.

John August Sutter was born Johann Augustus Suter in Switzerland in 1803. He married at the age of 23, fathered a family, ran up tremendous debts, and avoided prison only by abandoning his family and escaping to America. After five years traveling through the West and building up a fraudulent reputation as a military captain and a man of means, he arrived in California in 1839 and boldly announced plans to establish a great colony.

Sutter picked a spot for his colony at the junction of the American and Sacramento rivers. He cleared land, planted orchards and crops, established livestock herds, and pushed back the wilderness. He called his empire New Helvetia, in reference to the ancient name of his fatherland.

In 1841, Sutter bought Fort Ross from the Russians in an attempt to expand his empire. Unfortunately, he had little money and operated almost entirely on credit. The Fort Ross purchase brought his debts to the critical point, and crop failures in 1843 added to the load. To keep himself going, he mortaged his property, defaulted on payments to the Russians, forged checks, and sold his Native American slaves.

After James Marshall discovered gold in the tailrace of Sutter's partially completed mill, Sutter naively asked all his men to keep the event a secret so he could get some lumber cut and sold. At the same time, he tried to acquire mineral rights to the Coloma land. But the rights weren't granted, news of the discovery leaked out, and Sutter lost his big chance. Miners divided the Coloma lands, and squatters even carved up New Helvetia.

After stories of Sutter, both as a wealthy do-gooder and a debt-ridden despot, reached Europe, one of his sons decided to visit New Helvetia to get the facts. Young Augustus Sutter found his father in a scandalous situation, living the high life while the debts mounted higher. In a legal move to thwart Russian attempts to dispossess Sutter, all of New Helvetia was transferred into the son's name.

Young Sutter saved his father from destruction. At the suggestion of Sam Brannan (a Mormon miner who dramatically spread news of the gold discovery to San Francisco), he founded a new city named Sacramento and used the income from land sales to pay his father's debts. The fort was sold to raise more money, and Sutter and son moved their headquarters to a farm on the Feather River. Since the family finances were now in good shape, young Sutter sent for his mother and sister. But by the time they arrived, John had somehow managed to gain full control of the land and money.

Augustus left for Mexico, and with him went all semblance of order in the household. Sutter's xtravagances got the better of him again, and within a year he had lost all of his property and business interests. Even the farm had to be mortgaged to pay for lawyers, taxes, interest on loans, and personal expenses.

Without any means of support, Sutter retired to his farm to live a despondent life. He and his wife fled East when squatters burned down their ranch house. They settled in Lititz, Pennsylvania, where Sutter died on June 18, 1880.

Historic Attractions

Marshall Gold Discovery State Historic Park

P.O. Box 265
Coloma, CA 95613
916/622-3470

About 70 percent of the small town of Coloma lies wthin the 224-acre park that prserves the gold discovery site. Scattered among the grassy grounds are the Wah Hop Store (exhibits inside are typical of those used in Chinese shops during the Gold Rush), the Man Lee Store (another stone structure with a display of mining artifacts), a gunsmith's shop, a school, a period residence, an I.O.O.F. hall, several churches, and the mouldering ruins of a jail.

Buildings are marked for easy identification. Rangers on duty in the museum provide detailed maps of the park, showing all points of interest. A replica of the original gold nugget is displayed in the museum; the original belongs to the Smithsonian Institution.

On a hill behind the old town, an imposing bronze statue of James Marshall points to the site of the gold discovery. You can drive a side road up to the monument or take a short hike to Marshall's statue by way of his reconstructed cabin and an interesting old Catholic cemetery. *Open daily. Hot and crowded during summer; best in spring or fall. Day-use fee per vehicle includes museum entrance.*

Sutter's Mill

By far the most imposing structure in Coloma is the reconstruction of Sutter's Mill. It wasn't possible to rebuild the mill on the exact location of the original since the American River has altered its course substantially since 1848. But the rebuilders were able to follow the original construction techniques right down to the hand-hewn beams and mortise-and-tenon joints. The electrically powered sawmill operates regularly on weekends in fair weather. You can also watch ore being crushed at a nearby two-stamp mill.

Bronze statue of James Marshall, Coloma   Photo courtesy of Martin Litton

Diversions

Olde Coloma Theatre

Coloma State Park
916/626-5282

From approximately May through September, the Coloma Crescent Players present melodramas on weekend evenings in the small theater off Cold Springs Road. *Call for ticket information.*

River-running

A number of commercial operators run rafting and kayaking trips on the American River. Ask the park rangers for information.

Lodging

Coloma Country Inn

345 High Street
P.O. Box 502
Coloma, CA 95613
916/622-6919 **$$**

A restored 1850s Victorian charmer nestled among tree-studded lawns just above the park houses a seven-room country retreat (one two-bedroom suite) complete with wrap-around porch. The owners can make arrangements for whitewater raft trips or hot-air balloon rides after breakfast.

The Vineyard House

530 Cold Springs Road
P.O. Box 176
Coloma, CA 95613
916/622-2217 **$$**

Locals tell ghostly tales about this supposedly haunted Victorian inn across the street from the old Coloma Cemetery. Built in 1878 as a residence for a wealthy winemaker, the house has seven antique-furnished rooms (no private baths). A busy restaurant is on the first floor. The wine cellar houses a popular saloon and what is left of a jail cell. Behind the inn lies all that remains of the old winery.

Dining

Vineyard House Restaurant

Address and phone number
listed above **$**

A busy and attractive dining spot, the restaurant has seasonal menus that might include both chicken and dumplings and salmon with hollandaise sauce. Don't skip the free homemade bread pudding. *Breakfast, lunch, and dinner served Tuesday through Sunday in summer; schedule varies in winter.*

Side Trips

Lotus

Now off the beaten trail, the little hamlet of Lotus lives a quiet existence with only a few reminders of its early days. The schoolhouse, opened in 1869, is now a private residence. Atop a nearby hill, the small Uniontown Pioneer Cemetery (Lotus was first named Marshall and later Uniontown) contains headstones from the 1850s. The timbers for the brick building that housed Adam Lohry's General Store (right side of Lotus Road) were supposedly cut at Sutter's mill.

A campground about a mile beyond Lotus is a popular staging area for American River rafters.

North on Highway 49

The only building of interest in the former mining town of Pilot Hill is the three-story Bayley House, originally planned as a hotel for railroad passengers. The building became known as "Bayley's Folley" when the Central Pacific, which was supposed to pass within a half-mile of the hotel, chose another route at the last minute.

After Alonso Bayley finished the house in 1862, he tried to run it as a hotel, but he never enjoyed any success. The building was sold several times during the next 50 years and even operated as the headquarters of a cattle ranch. Today it stands as a stately reminder of a dream that collapsed.

The town got its name from the "pilot" fires burned on the highest hill to guide pathfinder John C. Fremont's party from the valley to the Sierra.

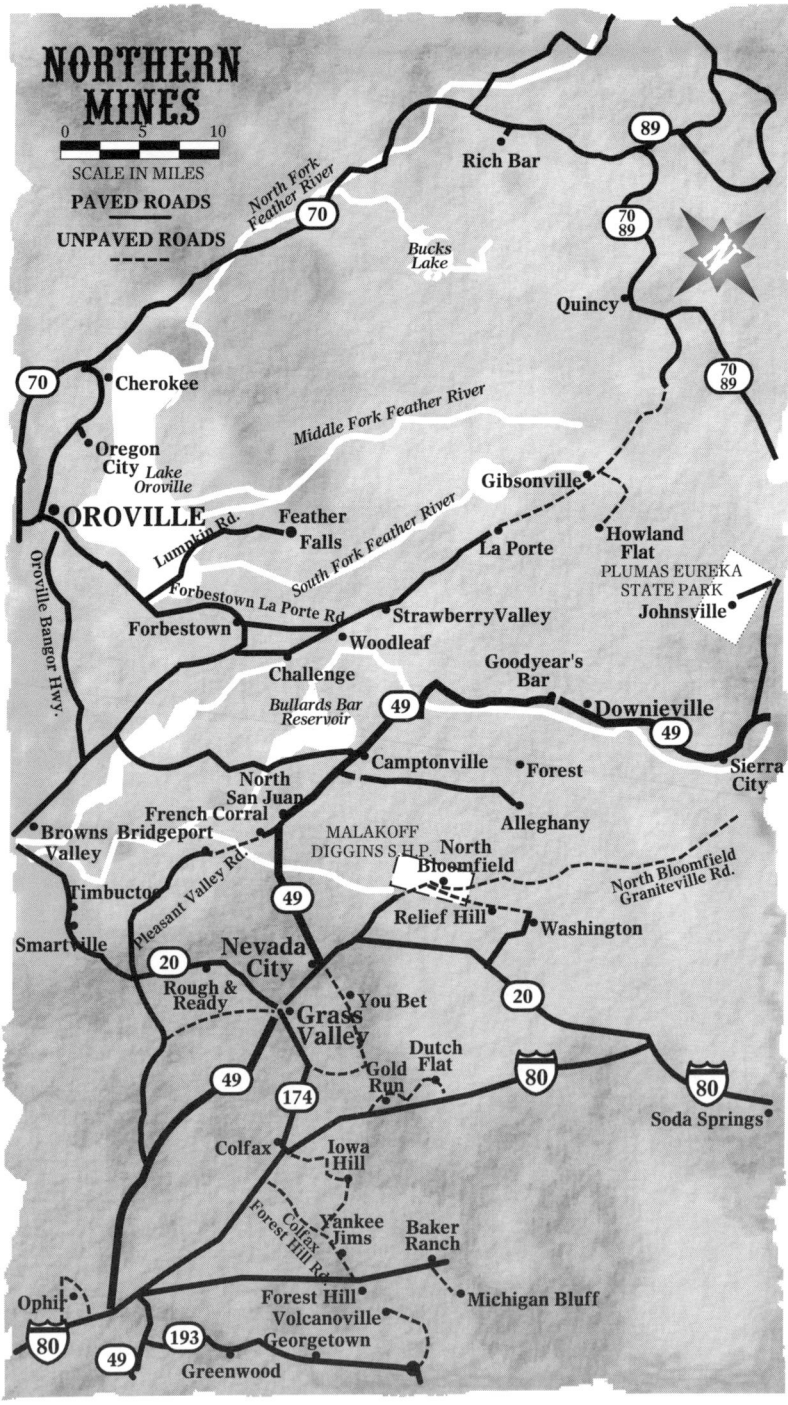

NORTHERN MINES

0   5   10
SCALE IN MILES
PAVED ROADS
UNPAVED ROADS
- - - - -

Rich Bar

89

70
89

North Fork Feather River

70

Bucks Lake

Quincy

70
89

70

Cherokee

Middle Fork Feather River

Oregon City *Lake Oroville*

Gibsonville

Howland Flat

OROVILLE

Feather Falls

La Porte

PLUMAS EUREKA STATE PARK

Johnsville

Lumpkin Rd.

South Fork Feather River

Forbestown La Porte Rd.

StrawberryValley

Forbestown

Woodleaf

Goodyear's Bar

Oroville Bangor Hwy.

Challenge

Bullards Bar Reservoir

49

Downieville

49

Camptonville

Forest

Sierra City

North San Juan

Alleghany

French Corral

Browns Valley

Bridgeport

MALAKOFF DIGGINS S.H.P.

North Bloomfield

Timbuctoo

Pleasant Valley Rd.

49

North Bloomfield Graniteville Rd.

Smartville

Relief Hill

Washington

20

Nevada City

Rough & Ready

You Bet

20

Grass Valley

Dutch Flat

49

174

Gold Run

80

80

Soda Springs

Colfax

Iowa Hill

Colfax Forest Hill Rd.

Yankee Jims

Baker Ranch

Ophir

Forest Hill

Michigan Bluff

80

49

193

Volcanoville

Georgetown

Greenwood

NORTHERN MINES

Although panning, sluicing, and dredging were the gold-mining methods first used by prospectors in the Northern Mines, hardrock quartz mining (underground mining) was developed in this region. The area is also the birthplace of the highly destructive hydraulic mining that washed away entire mountain ridges.

Scenery is spectacular throughout most of the Northern Mines. It's a land of tall pines, deep gullies, and high mountain ridges. You can picnic beside a waterfall on a back road to tiny Alleghany or patiently sift sands alongside a rushing river near Downieville, one of the spots recommended for gold panning. Except in midsummer, you may be the only tourist in many "almost" ghost towns.

Most of your wanderings off the main highways should be planned for summer, as side roads may be unpaved and often impassable because of winter snows and spring run-off. There are more choices for accommodations in the three largest towns in the Northern Mines—Auburn, Grass Valley, and Nevada City—but some unexpected gems for overnight stays lie only a little way off Highway 49.

Auburn

Interstate 80 bisects Auburn, the Gold Country's largest city. The historic Old Town is south of the highway; to the north lie most motels and restaurants. Once you reach the Old Town area (now preserved as a National Historic Landmark), it's easy to ignore the surrounding modernity. If you follow Highway 49 north, you can reach Old Town by turning west on Lincoln Way. From Interstate 80, the Old Town exit is clearly marked.

In the spring of 1848, Claude Chana (whose stone statue overlooks Old Town) and his gold seeking party set out from Sacramento for Sutter's Mill. The first night out they camped by a stream now known as Auburn Ravine. Chana tested the gravels for gold, and in his first pan found three sizable nuggets. This was evidence enough for the party, and, on May 16, 1848, they pitched tents and started mining operations.

During the summer of that year, the gravels at North Fork Dry Diggings (the camp's first name) yielded great wealth to those who took the effort to cart the pay dirt to the stream below. It was commonplace for a miner to wash out $1,000 to $1,500 a day. One account tells of four or five cartloads producing $16,000 in a single day. By 1850, 1,500 miners were busily digging in Auburn Ravine.

The little settlement became known as Woods' Dry Diggins when a soldier named John S. Woods made a profitable strike from his dry digging claim along the present western city limits. The name Auburn first appeared in November of 1849, and probably came from a large group of miners who had crossed the country with a Volunteer Regiment from Auburn, New York.

The busy little settlement became a county seat in 1850, probably because the town's population exceeded that of the rest of what was then Sutter County. When Placer County was formed the following year, Auburn retained the county seat.

After the surface placers were exhausted, quartz mining kept the town booming. However, it wasn't gold that built the modern city you find today. From its very earliest days, Auburn's location has made it a natural transportation center. It's also a convenient stop for motorists bound for Lake Tahoe and Reno.

Because the business district expanded up the hill over the years, the town's earliest buildings have been left relatively untouched by modern commerce. You can pick up a walking tour from the Auburn Area Chamber of Commerce (601 Lincoln Way) in the restored railroad station.

Many noteworthy buildings are found along Lincoln Way, Court Street, and Commercial Street. Note especially the whimsical four-story firehouse, the former Wells Fargo Office, and the post office that opened in 1849. The stone sculpture of town founder Claude Chana captures him with some of the nuggets he panned down in Auburn Ravine.

RATTLESNAKE DICK

In the early days of the Gold Rush, mining camps were lawless, with everybody who couldn't mine gold trying to pick it up one way or another. A few unsuccessful prospectors made their fortunes by robbing stages. Such a man was Rattlesnake Dick. Though he was occasionally captured and jailed, Dick always managed to escape, leaving local authorities considerably upset.

Once, a deputy from Auburn received word that Rattlesnake Dick and a friend were arriving in town on a stage from Nevada City. He waylaid the stage and attempted to place the men under arrest, but the outlaws boldly demanded to see his warrant first. While the diligent officer was looking through his pockets, Dick pulled out a gun and shot him. Before taking his leave, he also made a few unkind comments about "unfriendly Placer County."

Fittingly, Dick met his fate in Placer County. While riding boldly down the main street of Auburn, he was challenged by a posse and shot to death.

Historic Attractions

Placer County Courthouse

101 Maple Street
Auburn
916/889-6500

Though not really a Gold Rush building (it was completed in 1894), this imposing domed structure is located on the public square that served as the first public hanging yard and graveyard for the town. The first floor has been transformed into an intriguing museum that traces county history. Highlights include a holographic miner who pans for gold, a department store with ever-changing window displays, and Native American exhibits. *Open 10 A.M. to 4 P.M. Tuesday through Sunday except on holidays. Free admission.*

Photo courtesy of the Golden Chain Council

Placer County Courthouse, Auburn

Gold Country Museum

1273 High Street
Gold Country Fairgrounds
Auburn
916/889-4134

This large museum south of Old Town gives you a good look at area mining and early-day history. Visitors can walk through a mine shaft, observe a working model of a stamp mill, view a monitor nozzle, and find out how an assay office operated. Kids can try their luck at gold panning. *Open 10 A.M. to 3:30 P.M. Tuesday through Friday , 11 A.M. to 4 P.M. weekends. Admission $1 adults, 50 cents for children 6 to 16 and seniors. Ticket prices include admission to Bernhard Museum (see below).*

Bernhard Museum

291 Auburn-Folsom Road
near High Street
Auburn
916/889-4156

Though this house started out as the Traveler's Rest Hotel when it was built in 1851, it became the residence of viticulturist Benjamin Bernhard and his family in 1868. Visitors can take a guided tour through the large home and the outbuildings connected with the old winery. *Open 11 A.M. to 3 P.M. Tuesday through Friday, 10 A.M. to 4 P.M. weekends. Admission $1 adults, 50 cents for children 6 to 16 and seniors. Ticket prices include admission to the Gold Country Museum (see above).*

Diversions

Auburn State Recreation Area

East of downtown Auburn
916/885-4527

A network of trails make the American River canyons accessible to hikers, swimmers, picnickers, and gold panners. Rangers have information on several commercial white-water operators who run stretches of the river.

Lodging

Powers Mansion Inn

164 Cleveland Avenue
Auburn, CA 95603
916/885-1166 **$$**

This pretty pink inn in the heart of downtown Auburn was a showplace when it was built around the turn of the century. Antiques grace all 11 rooms (brass beds and private baths); the

Honeymoon Suite even boasts a heart-shaped tub for two. Rates include a full breakfast in the dining room.

Auburn Inn

1875 Auburn Ravine Road
Auburn, CA 95603
916/885-1800 **$$**

Its location off Interstate 80 and the attractive grounds make this 85-room, two-story motel a favorite with travelers. Amenities include a pool and spa, cable TV, and room phones. A coffee shop is nearby.

Dining

Latitudes

130 Maple Street, across
from the courthouse
Auburn
916/885-9535 **$**

This lovely Victorian house is now a popular purveyor of ethnic cuisine. Instead of a hamburger for lunch, try a Thai burrito stuffed with shrimp, sprouts, chiles, and rice. Dinner selections include fish and poultry dishes with an international flavor. *Open for lunch and dinner Wednesday through Sunday and Sunday brunch. Dinner reservations suggested.*

Madame Rouge

853 Lincoln Way
Auburn
916/888-7766 **$**

This nicely appointed restaurant is a welcome addition to Auburn's dining scene. The speciality is Mediterranean-style cuisine, but they also have steaks on the menu. The owner, a professional entertainer, will gladly sing while you dine. He sings by request only. *Open daily except Monday for lunch and dinner. Evening entertainment. Full bar. Reservations recommended.*

Headquarters House at Raspberry Hill

14500 Musso Road,
Bell Road exit off Interstate 80
Auburn
916/878-7595   **$**

Set amid pine trees, what was once the headquarters of the Dunipace Angus Ranch is now a casual, country-style restaurant specializing in chicken, seafood, and other entrees. *Open for lunch Wednesday-Saturday, dinner Wednesday-Sunday, and Sunday brunch. Full bar. Weekend dinner reservations suggested.*

Shanghai Restaurant

289 Washington Street
Auburn
916/823-2613   **$**

Service has been continuous since 1906 at this Chinese restaurant in the heart of Old Town. Even if you don't eat here, visit the historic bar-museum. *Open daily for lunch and dinner.*

Photo courtesy of the Golden Chain Council

Shanghai Restaurant, Old Town Auburn

Side Roads

Ophir

The richest diggings around Auburn were in the ravine west of town. Several camps grew up here during the 1850s, including Frytown, Virginiatown, Gold Hill, and Spanish Corral. The only one that is still recognizable is Spanish Corral, which was renamed Ophir when it reigned as the largest town in Placer County and was an important quartz-mining center. Now it is only a quiet crossroad. A marker describes the past, but fires and passing time have destroyed any Gold Rush remnants.

Forest Hill, Michigan Bluff, and Yankee Jims

Though not much remains of the once-prosperous gold camps in the foothills east of Auburn, a drive along Forest Hill Road is pleasant and scenic. The view of the American River from the spectacular bridge that spans the deep canyon is awe-inspiring.

An old cemetery is all that remains of the settlement of Todd's Valley southwest of Forest Hill. The region was named by Dr. F.W. Todd, an early settler. Todd started a store on his ranch in 1849. It soon became a stopping place for miners asking directions to new mining locations along the ridges around the area.

In the days of the gold craze, two stage robbers were apprehended and summarily hung from a nearby tree. Their bodies rest just outside the cemetery's fenced enclosure, as they were deemed unfit to lie within the sacred grounds. Some 60 unmarked graves, believed to be those of early miners, receive careful attention each May when volunteers clean up the premises.

The former mining camp of Forest Hill (now spelled Foresthill) lies on a ridge between Shirttail Canyon and the Middle Fork of the American River. Gold was discovered in 1850, but the boom really started when the Jenny Lind mine opened in 1852. This famous mine produced over a million dollars worth of gold by 1880, and the area around it produced in excess of 10 million dollars' worth.

Shirttail Canyon got its name when two miners prospecting along a creek walked downstream to avoid an obstruction which blocked their view. Rounding the point, they were surprised to

THE BELL OF ST. JOSEPH'S

In 1860, Forest Hill, heavily populated by hundreds of Irishmen laying track for the Central Pacific Railroad, had a small church but no resident priest. Young James Cullin, graduate of All Hallows College in Dublin, Ireland, learned of their need and volunteered for the job, arriving in 1863. A tireless and dedicated priest, he held services in towns all around the area.

One of Father Cullin's parishioners heard of a bell for sale in San Francisco, brought there by traders. It had been cast for a Greek Orthodox Church in Boston, but, by the time it arrived, that church was unable to buy it. The opportunistic traders sent it around Cape Horn to California. When Forest Hill's miners, railroaders, and other interested Catholics and Protestants heard about the bell, they collected $3,500 and bought it in the name of Father Cullin.

It took six horses, about a hundred men, and a struggle all the way to get the bell to Forest Hill. Then it was discovered St. Joseph's Catholic Church wasn't strong enough to support the four-ton bell, so a tower had to be built next to the church. Though it took two men to ring the great bell, the sound carried for 20 miles.

The old church burned in 1952, but the bell still stands atop a monument.

see a solitary prospector standing at the edge of the water clad only in a shirt. When the men met, the intruders asked the miner what the place was called. Glancing down at his bare legs and realizing his ludicrous appearance, the miner laughed heartily and answered, "Don't know any name for it yet, but we might as well call it Shirttail as anything else."

A collection of frame-sided, tin-roofed buildings at the end of Forest Hill Road and an old Chinese cemetery are all that remain of Michigan Bluff, an area best remembered for the extensive hydraulic mining which tore away surrounding mountainsides. Until the monitors were muzzled in 1858, bullion worth $100,000 was shipped from the area every month starting in 1853.

The first mining camp, then named Michigan City, was half a mile away from the present location. It was moved higher on the brow of Sugar Loaf Hill when the town's building foundations were undermined by the furious hydraulicking. Leland Stanford, who later founded Stanford University, operated a store here between 1853 and 1855.

From Foresthill, a twisting road leads to the ghost town of Yankee Jims, which was at one time Placer County's largest mining camp. The town sprang into being under strange circumstances, but the story is a credible one.

Yankee Jim, who was not a Yankee but an Australian, was a low character. Rather than dig wash the gravels of the American River, he stole horses. And nothing was lower than a horse thief, who, if caught, was instantly strung up. The old boy was good at his profession, however, and might have gone along indefinitely if one of his victims hadn't found his horse (and others) hidden in a corral on a remote ridge.

Yankee Jim hightailed it out of the country just in time to save his neck, which was sort of a shame because it wasn't much later that a miner wandered into the old corral to do a bit of prospecting and found the ground was rich in free gold. A crowded camp mushroomed up and a fortune was taken from the diggings, a fortune that could have been Jim's, if it had occurred to him to try his hand at a little honest labor.

Detour to Dutch Flat

Rather than proceeding to Grass Valley on Highway 49, you might consider a visit to the captivating community of Dutch Flat, 29 miles east of Auburn via Interstate 80. It's one of the most charming towns in the Northern Mines, and one of the few Gold Country communities that has not suffered a serious fire. Because of this blessing and its off-the-beaten-path location, a significant number of old buildings have survived, including a hotel (no longer accepting guests), the I.O.O.F. and Masonic halls, the Methodist church, and a number of residences.

Children (and adults) will enjoy peering through the windows of appropriately named Hearse House, visiting the small museum, and wandering among headstones in the pioneer cemetery above town. Adjoining it is a Chinese burial ground, almost hidden among tall pines. (When possible, the bodies of most Chinese were removed at later dates and returned to China for proper burial.)

Dutch Flat sprang into existence when Joseph Dorenbach, a German miner, and his countrymen started washing the gravels around the area in 1851. From 1854 to 1883, it was one of the state's principal placer-mining communities. Millions of dollars in gold were taken out; one nugget alone was worth more than $5,000. The "diggins" lay over the hill in rugged man-made canyons about 100 feet north of the town site.

Dutch Flat School, Placer County   Photo courtesy of Martin Litton

Until the railroad pushed its way farther up the mountains to the town of Cisco, Dutch Flat was an important stage stop on both the Donner Pass and Henness Pass routes. At the height of its prosperity, the town supported two hotels and dozens of other businesses.

Roadside rests on each side of Interstate 80 at Gold Run (west of Dutch Flat) display antique mining machinery. Those artifacts and the little shiny-roofed Union church are the only mementos left of Gold Run, a town that became rich during hydraulic mining days. The church was one of many buildings in the Gold Country financed by miners' contributions.

Instead of returning to Auburn to catch Highway 49 north, you can follow State 174 to Grass Valley from Colfax. The highway traces the route of a toll road used in the early 1900s. Colfax, named after Schuyler Colfax, Ulysses S. Grant's vice-president, turned from mining to shipping after the Central Pacific Railroad reached the town in September, 1865.

Off State 174, a narrow, bumpy gravel road (U-Bet Road) takes you past two former hydraulic mining camps, Red Dog and You Bet. All that's left of the once-flourishing town of Red Dog are a few frame buildings and a small cemetery.

Grass Valley

Grass Valley is a town of golden memories, many of them carefully preserved in historic mining museums and parks that impress even the most sophisticated tourist. But, in spite of its well-defined past, the town that has modernized. First-time visitors may find it amusing to see elegant Victorian homes overlooking tract houses, shopping centers abutting mining tailings, and narrow, winding streets ending abruptly at the wide freeway.

It was in Grass Valley that gold mining hit its peak as an industry. This was not a legendary ground where grizzled miners uncovered big nuggets, but it was the area where big money and big machinery moved in to take as much gold as efficiently as possible. The most important ruins" left around town are not small brick businesses or quaint Chinese quarters, but headframes and inclined shafts from the mining complexes that once employed thousands of men.

When the big mining companies moved in, they also attracted important suppliers and peripheral industries, so Grass Valley possessed a broad economic base that was very rare in the Gold Country. The business of deep quartz mining started here, and the hit-and-miss methods of adventurous prospecting were replaced by industrial techniques that required brains, know-how, and financial backing instead of luck and brawn.

The first big strike, however, came about much as it did in many other gold camps—just by accident. The surface diggings in this area were not rich, so only a few of the frenzied prospectors even bothered to set up camp in 1849. One of those who did try his luck on the edges of Boston Ravine was George Knight (or McKnight, depending on the history you read), who was destined to change the area's fortunes overnight.

The story goes that Knight was out chasing his wandering cow in the moonlight when he stubbed his toe on a rocky outcropping. The stumble knocked loose a piece of rock, and Knight noticed the glitter of shining metal. He forgot about his cow, took the rock home, and crushed it. A few minutes' work with the gold pan revealed that the rock was gold-bearing quartz.

News of the discovery brought miners in droves, and by summer the Gold Hill Company had built a mill near the point where the toe-stubbing took place. Between 1850 and 1857 this mine produced gold worth four million dollars. Other companies followed: Empire, North Star, Pennsylvania, Idaho-Maryland, and Brunswick were located within a mile or two of town. Hundreds of miles of tunnels and shafts were dug beneath Grass Valley and its neighbor to the north, Nevada City, and mining continued well into the 1950s. The Idaho-Maryland Mine averaged two million dollars per year even during the war years.

The century-old Empire Mine is now a state park. It operated until 1956, but was shut down because the operating costs were too high when compared to the stabilized price of gold (then $35 an ounce). Once the Cornish pumps stopped operating, water flooded its tunnels. Today the water level is approximately 150 feet below the ground surface.

A huge fire in 1855 (probably the most disastrous of the many that ravaged Gold Rush camps) destroyed the 300-odd frame buildings that made up the original community of Grass Valley. It is said that this fire inspired the development of the characteristic heavy masonry walls and iron shutters that now typify a large part of Mother Lode architecture.

The romance of early mining still clings to Grass Valley, conjuring up images of famous historic characters who once strolled these very streets: Mark Twain, Bret Harte, George Hearst, and many more. A plaque at the refurbished Holbrooke Hotel (see Lodging below) commemorates the visits of four U.S. presidents.

Make your first stop at 248 Mill Street, corner of Walsh Street. This house where sultry entertainer Lola Montez lived is now home to the Nevada County Chamber of Commerce. Some of Lola's period pieces still occupy one room of the small house. Here you can pick up a guide to other historic sites in and around the city.

Historic Attractions

Empire Mine State Historic Park

10791 E. Empire Street
Grass Valley
1 mile east of Highway 49
916/273-8522

The sprawling Empire Mine was California's oldest, largest, and richest hardrock mine and the third most productive in the United States. From its beginnings in 1850 to its closure more than a century later (in 1956), an estimated 5.8 million ounces of gold were extracted from some 367 miles of underground shafts.

The state purchased the 777 acres in 1975 for 1.2 million dollars, giving visitors an unequaled opportunity to learn about the techniques of quartz mining and to imagine just what it was like back in the days when stamp mills pounded thunderously around the clock. A map shows the locations of the mine shaft and restored surface buildings, the Bourn Cottage (the owner's mansion) and nearby clubhouse, and the 10 miles of hiking trails. *Admission $2 adults, $1 children ages 6 to 12. Open daily in summer; weekends in the off-seasons. Films in the visitor center; tours. Hiking, cycling, and picnicking areas.*

COUSIN JACKS

As word spread to England that gold had been found in California and underground mining had begun, miners from the tin and copper mines of Cornwall flocked to the Mother Lode to share their experience and expertise—and to, hopefully, gain in some of the wealth. Cornishmen provided the bulk of the labor force at the Empire and other large mines around Grass Valley from the late 1870s until 1956. Of particular note was the Cornish contribution to the system of steam pumps that kept the water from seeping into the deep shafts.

Mine owners, impressed by the skills of their Cornish workers, were always sympathetic (and amused) when told of a "Cousin Jack" back home who would be interested in coming to California, if passage could be provided. So many "Cousin Jacks" were hired by the late 1800s that Grass Valley's population was almost 85 percent Cornish.

Along with "Cousin Jack" came "Cousin Jenny," who was skilled in producing tasty meat-and-vegetable pies. Known as "pasties," they served as meals for miners during their shifts underground. Versions of the original recipes are still served in Grass Valley shops.

The Cornish were also known for their sweet singing voices, and listening to a Cornish Choir at Christmas was a favorite holiday treat. Today's visitors to Grass Valley can still enjoy Cornish food and music during the city's Cornish Christmas celebrations, held on the four Fridays before the holiday. For additional information on the festivities, call (916) 272-8315.

North Star Mining Museum and Pelton Wheel Exhibit

Mill Street at Allison Ranch Road
Grass Valley
916/273-4255

A visit to the educational mining museum in Boston Ravine is a "must." Formerly the Power Station for the North Star Mine, it is the home of the world's largest Pelton wheel (see Glossary of Mining Terms). The enlarged powerhouse displays a grand collection of mining artifacts. *Open 11 A.M. to 5 P.M. daily except Monday from spring until early autumn. Donations suggested.*

Grass Valley Museum

Mount St. Mary's Convent
and St. Joseph's Chapel
410 South Church
Grass Valley
916/272-4725

High brick walls and lawns surround the venerable complex (built in 1863) that was once home to an orphanage and elementary school. The middle floor of the old convent houses the city's pioneer museum. The cemetery on the grounds dates back to 1852. *Grounds open daily; museum open daily except Monday in summer, Tuesday through Friday the rest of the year. Donations accepted. Thrift shop.*

Video History Museum

415 Central Avenue
Memorial Park
Grass Valley
916/274-1126

Using still photos and old movies, this small museum has created an historical video of life in Grass Valley and neighboring Nevada City. It gives visitors a good look at the region's early mining, logging, and transportation. Also of interest are Native American, Chinese, railroad, fire department, and World War II artifacts. *Open daily except Wednesday from 11 A.M. to 4 P.M. in summer, by appointment the rest of the year. Donations accepted.*

Lodging

Holbrooke Hotel

212 W. Main Street
Grass Valley, CA 95945
916/273-1353 **$$**

Mark Twain, Black Bart, Lola Montez, and Lotta Crabtree are only a few of the famous (or infamous) people who have slept in this downtown beauty. The restored hotel is well-known for its popular bar and restaurant, and offers 28 rooms, both upstairs and in its Victorian annex. Touches of yesterday and today blend happily: TVs hide in armoires and claw-footed tubs enliven modern baths. Many rooms have private balconies. Continental breakfast is served in the library.

Murphy's Inn

318 Neal Street
Grass Valley, CA 95945
916/273-6873 **$$**

Once the 19th-century estate of Edward Coleman, owner of the North Star and Idaho mines, this elegant (and expensive) inn has eight delightfully decorated rooms and baths. There are also a topiary garden accented by whispering fountains, a fish pond, and a 2,000-year-old sequoia on the grounds. The homemade breakfast is delicious.

Swan-Levine House

328 Church Street
Grass Valley, CA 95945
916/272-1873 **$$**

This small former hospital is today an eclectic inn. The baths of the four guest rooms have both showers and Victorian tubs. Book the Bunk Room if you're bringing the family. A communal breakfast is served in the kitchen.

Golden Ore Bed and Breakfast Inn

448 S. Auburn Street
Grass Valley, CA 95945
916/272-6872 **$$**

Obviously named with tongue in cheek, this pleasant six-room inn (three rooms with private baths) successfully combines the past (antiques) and the present (skylights and decks). A large breakfast gets you off to a good start.

Dining

Tofanelli's

302 W. Main Street
Grass Valley
916/272-1468 **$**

This inexpensive cafe with a simple decor serves everything from vegetarian specialties to homemade desserts. Breakfast burritos and raspberry chicken are popular items. *Open daily for breakfast, lunch, and dinner. Patio dining available. Beer and wine.*

Pepper's

151 Mill Street
Grass Valley
916/272-7780 **$**

Tucked away in the one-time Union newspaper building, this restaurant offers Southwestern and Mexican selections. Depart from the traditional and try a fresh fruit chimichanga with ice cream for dessert. *Open for lunch Tuesday through Saturday, dinner daily. Beer and wine.*

Owl Tavern

134 Mill Street
Grass Valley
916/274-1144 **$**

Miners would feel right at home in this brick-walled tavern designed to recreate the Gold Rush theme. The menu selections are rib-sticking, and bar is popular with locals. *Open daily for lunch and dinner. Bar.*

Mrs. Dubblebee's Pasties

251-C South Auburn Street
Grass Valley
916/272-7700 $

This combination bakery-cafe is a supplier of the town's specialty, the beef-and-potato pies called "pasties" that were carried by the Cornish miners for lunch. *Open daily for light lunch and early dinner.*

Side Trip

Rough and Ready

A quiet little village that belies its name, Rough and Ready lies about four miles west of Grass Valley on Highway 20. It was founded by a band of Mexican War veterans who took the name from their ex-commander, General Zachary Taylor, "Old Rough and Ready."

Rough and Ready's greatest fame comes from its secession from the Union in 1850 in protest over a miners' tax. The town actually returned to the United States after a few months, but the rebellion was not officially ended until 1948. Peace was finally made with the federal government so that a post office could be opened.

One of the town's most famous incidents reflects the temper of the Gold Rush times. It seems that an unlucky miner was being buried with a regular funeral and all the trimmings, when one of the "mourners" suddenly noticed some gold in the freshly turned earth at the gravesite. Before the preacher could finish the service, claims had been staked around the coffin and the miners had started to work.

During the 1850s there were more than 300 frame buildings in this town. Today three of Rough and Ready's oldest landmarks are the schoolhouse, an I.O.O.F. Hall, and a blacksmith's shop. The Old Toll House, which charged from 25 cents to $3 to pass through, depending on your load, now extracts revenues from tourists by the sale of antiques.

It was at weather-worn Fippin's Smithy that little Lotta Crabtree, a young Gold Rush singer and dancer, made her first appearance.

THE PELTON WHEEL

One of the most important inventions to come out of the California Gold Rush was the Pelton wheel, a super-efficient waterwheel employing modern turbine principles to produce useful power for mining. The inventor was Lester Pelton of Camptonville, California, who patented his wheel in 1878.

Most mining machinery used late in the last century and early in this one was powered by compressed air. The use of internal-combustion or steam engines in the mines would have asphyxiated the miners, and water in the shafts and tunnels made the use of electric motors uncertain and hazardous.

The Pelton wheel was instantly recognizable by the large number of relatively small buckets affixed to the rim. Each bucket was a single casting or forging divided by a central ridge into two bowl-like scoops. A jet of water delivered from a high-pressure nozzle aimed dead center at the bucket was split by the dividing ridge and turned into two powerful reverse jets that drove the bucket forward.

You can see one of the biggest Pelton wheels ever made at the Nevada County Historical Mining Museum in Grass Valley's Boston Ravine. Installed in 1896 by the North Star Mining Company, the wheel is 30 feet in diameter, weighs about 10 tons, and operated for 40 years. It steadily cranked the massive connecting rods of two 30-inch and two 18-inch pistons to power the mine's hoists, pumps, triphammers, drills, and forges, delivering compressed air through 800 feet of six-inch pipe at a pressure of 90 pounds per square inch. You can imagine the strength and fine balance that had to be built into the wheel when you realize that, at normal operating speed of 65 revolutions per minute, the rim was moving at the rate of 70 miles per hour.

Nevada City

Nevada City has acquired a well-deserved reputation as one of the most charming of the Gold Rush towns. A wealth of delightful inns and eating spots make this a good base from which to explore the countryside. Malakoff Diggins State Historic Park, site of an impressive example of hydraulic mining, lies only a few miles to the northeast, and California's last covered bridge spans the Yuba River to the west.

Purists claim that turning Highway 49 into a freeway through Nevada City did irreparable damage. They may be right. Even though very few old buildings were torn down to make way for the freeway, the town's ambience of gracious elegance was greatly diminished by the presence of a mass of concrete.

But Nevada City still manages to overcome this streak of modernity with great dignity. The entire downtown district is a National Historic Landmark. Carefully preserved pieces of antiquity now house shops, restaurants, theaters, galleries, and museums.

Church spires reach high above pine-clad hills and roof tops on the slopes of Deer Creek Ravine. Winding residential streets are lined with sugar maples that blaze with autumn color. The architecture of the genteel Victorian buildings is both eye-catching and memory-provoking: broad balconies and roof turrets, mullioned windows and widows' walks, garden gazebos and picket fences.

The best way to explore is on foot. You can pick up a self-guided walking tour brochure from the Nevada City Chamber of Commerce (132 Main Street) that gives information on the most intriguing buildings and directions to museums and other points of interest. The foot-weary can board horse-drawn carriages outside Friar Tucks's restaurant or the National Hotel for tours of downtown or of the residential sections.

Nevada City is one of the earliest towns in the Northern Mines. The city sprang up when miners started working the placers along Deer Creek in 1849. It was known by various names, including Caldwell's Upper Store, Deer Creek Dry Diggin's, Coyoteville, and finally Nevada. The "City" was added later when the neighboring state appropriated the town's name for its own.

Like other Gold Rush towns, Nevada City started as a camp, became a tent village, and evolved into a tinder-box town of wooden buildings. Razed by fire, it was rebuilt, burned, was rebuilt again, and burned again in 1856. It was this last conflagration that caused the citizens to form fire companies and build three good firehouses. Two are still in use by the Nevada City fire department, and the third houses an historical museum.

Broad Street is the main thoroughfare of town. There stand the Nevada Theatre (now restored to a legitimate stage), the National Hotel (see Lodging below), the New York Hotel, the Methodist church (1864), and the red brick Firehouse No. 2. Farther out, on West Broad Street, is the pioneer cemetery.

The old Chinatown, on Commercial Street, is still marked by a few 1860s buildings. Coyote Street is named after "coyote

Photo courtesy of Dave Carter

Firehouse No. 2, Nevada City

holes," small shafts used to get at the gold deposits buried deep in the gravels of old river beds.

Nevada City's penchant for preservation is quite a change from the days when the miners were so eager for wealth they kept city streets torn up. A story is told of an angry merchant demanding that a miner stop digging up the street. The miner refused, stating there was no law to prevent him from such an action. "Then I'll make a law," replied the indignant merchant, producing his revolver. Destruction of the streets is said to have halted almost immediately.

Historic Attractions

South Yuba Canal Building, Ott's Assay Office

132 Main Street
Nevada City
916/265-2692

These two adjoining structures are Nevada City's oldest business buildings. The South Yuba Canal Building (1855) was first a drug store and later the offices for the state's largest water system. Ott's Assay Office (1857) is the place where James J. Ott assayed the ore samples in 1859 that led to Nevada's famous Comstock Lode silver rush.

Firehouse No. 1

214 Main Street
Nevada City
916/265-5468

When the Victorian bell tower and gingerbread trim were added, this venerable firehouse (built in 1861) became a photographer's delight. The fire company has been replaced by the Nevada County Historical Society Museum, which offers some unusual looks at life around the time of the Gold Rush. *Open daily from 11 A.M. to 4 P.M. April through October, closed Wednesday the rest of the year. Donations welcome.*

Miners Foundry Cultural Center

325 Spring Street
Nevada City
916/265-5040

The foundry that started operations in this building in 1856 made machinery for gold mines and other early industries, and produced the first Pelton water wheel in 1878. Memorabilia can be spotted on a stroll through the complex. The complex's tin-sided former garage now houses the Nevada City Winery, a reincarnation of an early winery that stood near here. Daily wine tastings are held in the afternoons.

Bridgeport Covered Bridge

Near Penn Valley
and French Corral.

Two miles southwest of French Corral stands the longest (230 feet) remaining single-span covered bridge in the West. Lumbermill owner David I. Wood built the wooden bridge in 1862 after floods washed out all the crossings on the South Fork of the Yuba River. For its first 39 years, the bridge was a turnpike toll crossing for wagons carrying freight and supplies to the Northern Mines and the Comstock Lode diggings in Nevada. It became a public road crossing in 1901, and was in use until declared unsafe in 1971, when it was closed to vehicular traffic. The state has since given the span historical landmark status.

Malakoff Diggins State Historic Park

North Bloomfield Road
27 miles northeast of Nevada City
via Highway 49 and Tyler Foote Crossing Road
916/265-2740

Malakoff Diggins were the scene of the biggest hydraulic mining operation in the world between 1866 and 1884. This type of mining was halted as the result of an important early anti-pollution court decision. The Diggins themselves have gone from being the Gold Rush Country's biggest mining scar to becoming a scenic wonder.

Park headquarters are in North Bloomfield, a town now deserted save for a few residents and park personnel. North Bloomfield was once called "Humbug" in honor of an imaginative, hard-drinking miner who lured dozens of prospectors to the area with his wild stories about gold-bearing gravels.

Many of the town's clapboard buildings have been restored. The pharmacy, saloon, and general store are still furnished and stocked as though ready for business. Cummins Hall (a former town center with a saloon in front) houses the visitor center. St. Columcille's Catholic Church, built in 1860 and moved here in 1971 from Birchville (near French Corral), started life as a training headquarters for the Bridgeport Union Guard.

In 1971, one of the old hydraulic nozzles was tested for use in the North Bloomfield Homecoming celebration that takes place each June. It lived up to its destructive reputation by washing away a part of the town's only sidewalk.

Day use fee. Museum open daily in summer, weekends in the spring and fall. Campground (reserve sites through MISTIX, 800/444-7275), and rustic cabins (reserve through the park).

Malakoff Diggins State Historic Park   Photo courtesy of Martin Litton

LOLA AND LOTTA—
TWO GLAMOROUS PERFORMERS

Lola Montez

There are no more famous names in the history of the Northern Mines than those of Lola Montez and Lotta Crabtree. They injected an element of glamour into the tedious routine of the mining camps, and stories about the flashy pair were easy to come by and often repeated.

Born Eliza Gilbert in Ireland in 1818, Lola Montez was a sensation in Europe during the 1840s, both for her theatrical talents and her personal life. She was the mistress of Ludwig of Bavaria for two years and later presided over soirees honoring the continent's foremost literary and artistic figures. Franz Liszt, George Sand, Victor Hugo, and Alexander Dumas were among her intimates.

Lotta Crabtree

Lola embarked on a tour of America in 1852 and eventually arrived in San Francisco the following year. Though her famous beauty and notoriety were admired, her mediocre dancing talents (even the exotic Spider Dance) were somewhat disappointing to jaded San Franciscans. She received an even harsher reception at performances in Sacramento and Marysville, and finally decided to retire in Grass Valley. She moved into a house at 248 Mill Street (home now to the Nevada County Chamber of Commerce). Lola threw big parties and gave occasional performances for local crowds. She also kept grizzly bears and monkeys for pets.

The Crabtree family lived just down the block from the Montez home, and one day little Lotta stopped to chat. The bubbling, irrepressible little girl caught the aging beauty's fancy, and Lola began to teach her little friend songs and dances. Lotta learned very quickly and was soon performing for Miss Montez's guests. Legend has it that Lola took the talented 7-year-old with her on a trip to Rough and Ready, where Lotta gave her first public performance on top of the anvil in Fippin's Smithy while the talented blacksmith pounded out an accompaniment with his hammer.

About a year after Lola and Lotta first met, the Crabtrees moved to La Porte, where Lotta was a smash success in a performance at a local tavern. The miners showered the stage with coins and nuggets, and Lotta was launched on a busy and very successful career. She toured the mines for years, often in grueling one-night stands, and built a huge following. Finally, she went to San Francisco for successful engagements, to New York in 1864, and on to international fame. Lotta retired at an early age and lived gracefully until 1924. At the time of her death, her estate totaled $4 million.

Fate was not so kind to her teacher. Lola Montez grew weary of retirement and went on tour to Australia in 1855. She failed there and returned to the United States to try her hand at lecturing—still another failure. Her health began to give out, and once-wealthy Lola Montez spent a miserable final few years before passing away in New York at the age of 43. The year was 1861, just about the time that Lotta Crabtree began her career.

Diversions

Deer Creek Miners Trail

Nevada City

Pick up a guide for this short walk along Deer Creek at the trailhead beside the Broad Street freeway exit. The brochure lists six stations along the trail and describes what it was like to prospect for gold in Nevada City.

Gold Panning tours

Bridgeport on the South Yuba River
Malakoff Diggins State Historic Park
Call 916/432-2546 for the Bridgeport ranger station
916/265-2740 for Malakoff Diggins

Guided half-day, full-day, and overnight gold panning tours are available at several sites in Nevada County. You can also check with the Chamber of Commerce office for tour listings.

Lodging

In addition to motel-type accommodations, a dozen or so of Nevada City's historic homes have been transformed into small inns. Rates usually include breakfast for two. Some of the inns welcome children. Only a sampling of lodging is listed below; for a complete choice, call (800) 655-NJOY. When you need accommodations on short notice, call the Innkeepers' Association at (916) 477-6634.

The Red Castle

109 Prospect Street,
Nevada City, CA 95959
916/265-5135 **$$**

This inn was one of the state's first bed and breakfasts. It's still one of the best. Built in 1860 by a wealthy mine owner, the four-story, red brick architectural gem atop Prospect Hill simply drips with gingerbread trim. All seven antique-rich rooms have private verandas or garden terraces. A bountiful buffet breakfast is served in the parlor.

MADAME MOUSTACHE

One of the most colorful characters in early Nevada City history (or, for that matter, all Gold Country history) was Eleanor Dumont. She arrived in Nevada City one day in 1854, young, charming, well-dressed, of polite demeanor, and proper in every way except one: she was a professional gambler.

Madame Dumont opened a vingt-et-un (blackjack) parlor that became the talk of the mines. For two years she dealt the game to willing Nevada City miners, but as the surface deposits began to peter out, business slowed. In 1856, Dumont moved on.

Eleanor had acquired a nickname before she left town—Madame Moustache. The name, which followed her as she traveled from camp to camp, was prompted by the dark downy growth on her lip, and it seemed to sum up the lack of respect that the miners felt as the years tarnished the once-bright young woman.

No one is quite sure where Madame Moustache went. Legend has it she traveled all over the West from one boom town to the next, always gambling, always dealing the same game. Twenty-five years after she first stepped off the stage in Nevada City, she was found dead near Bodie, having committed suicide.

Grandmere's Inn

449 Broad Street
Nevada City, CA 95959
916/265-4660 **$$$**

Susan B. Anthony visited this three-story Colonial frequently when it was owned by Senator and Mrs. Aaron Sargeant, both of whom were suffragette supporters. The meticulously restored seven-room inn is conveniently located steps away from downtown.

The Marsh House

254 Boulder Street
Nevada City, CA 95959
916/265-5709   **$$$**

This dignified 1873 Italiante mansion and four-bedroom carriage house are situated amid a broad expanse of manicured lawns and lovely gardens. Opulently furnished with lumber baron Marsh's family heirlooms, two of the six rooms have fireplaces. All are on the expensive side.

The National Hotel

211 Broad Street
Nevada City, CA 95959
916/265-4551   **$$**

A contender for the claim of the oldest continuously operated hotel west of the Rockies, this historic downtown landmark was built between 1854 and 1857. Though not as elegant as they were when Lola and Lotta were part of the passing parade, the 43 rooms (each with a private bath) are comfortable. Enjoy cocktails in a saloon where gold dust was once the medium of exchange. Meals are served in the Victorian Dining Room.

The Northern Queen Inn

40 Railroad Avenue
Nevada City, CA 95959
916/265-5824   **$$**

This modern 86-room motel (pool and Jacuzzi) on 16 wooded acres along Gold Run Creek includes a few cottages with wood-burning stoves. The 1910 steam locomotive and electric car next door (on the original site of the Nevada County Narrow Gauge Railroad) occasionally take visitors on short runs.

Washington Hotel

15432 Washington Road
P.O. Box 32
Washington, CA 95986
916/265-4364 **$$**

This historic 12-room hotel, bar, and cafe stands on the banks of the South Yuba River in the tiny town of Washington, which is off Highway 20 east of Nevada City.

Dining

Nevada City offers more dining choices than most Gold Country towns. Travelers will find a range of cuisines, including Japanese (***Minami Japanese Restaurant***, 311 Broad Street), Mexican (***The Mexican Inn***, 401 Commercial Street), Italian (***Cirino's Restaurant***, 309 Broad Street), French (***Country Roses***, 300 Commercial Street), and vegetarian (***Earth Song***, Argall Way).

Potager's at Selaya

320 Broad Street
Nevada City
916/265-5697 **$$**

Potager's is one of the best bets for gourmet cuisine in the Mother Lode. This very popular restaurant offers a lengthy list of entrees plus some creative appetizers and desserts. The deli outlet around the corner (***Gourmet Food To Go***) is open for lunch on weekdays. *Dinner only Tuesday through Sunday. Weekend reservations suggested.*

Friar Tuck's

111 North Pine Street
Nevada City
916/265-9093 **$**

This menu of this lively dinner house includes fondue, fish, and steak. Singers and a variety of musicians entertain guests most evenings. *Open daily for dinner. Bar. Weekend reservations suggested.*

The Bouzy Rouge
203 York Street
Nevada City
916/265-9795 $
Friendly and fun, this Victorian-style dining room has singing waiters in addition to its American and Mediterranean-style food. *Open Wednesday through Sunday from 5 P.M. Reservations recommended.*

Side Roads

Highway 20 to Washington

This old settlement nestles in the canyon of the South Fork of the Yuba River. The town is surrounded by boulders piled up over a century ago by miners searching for gold. Two stone buildings (one with the date 1867 carved into its keystone) once acted as general stores. The historic Washington Hotel & Restaurant (see Lodging) is the only hostelry on the river. To get there, follow Highway 20 for 13 miles to Washington Road.

Numerous mining camps once located up and down the banks of the South Fork of the Yuba River are only colorful names today: Keno Bar, Jackass Flat, Lizard Flat, and Brass Wire Bar.

A dirt track leads to the site of Relief Hill, a few miles northwest of Washington. Long abandoned, the once-thriving town was first settled in 1853. Only a few frame shacks mark its location today. It is believed that the second relief party sent out to aid the Donner party met the refugees and their rescuers near here.

Relief Hill marker   Photo courtesy of Martin Litton

Pleasant Valley Road to French Corral and Bridgeport

A paved side road off Highway 49 (Pleasant Valley Road) leads to French Corral, a little town named for a Frenchman who built a corral for his mules here in 1849. The area enjoyed brief prosperty as a center for placer mining. The Milton Mining and Water Company established the state's first cross-country phone here in 1877, linking its headquarters in French Corral with French Lake, 58 miles away. The brick Wells Fargo building and the community center (originally built as a hotel and later used as a schoolhouse) both date back to the 1850s.

Bridgeport Bridge, two miles southwest of French Corral at the South Fork of the Yuba River, was built in 1862 as a toll crossing for the miners' freight and supplies. The shingle-sided bridge (now closed to vehicle travel) is the longest single span in the West.

Community Hall, French Corral   Photo courtesy of Martin Litton

North on Highway 49

Beyond Nevada City, Highway 49 wends its way north, dipping in and out of heavily forested river canyons. It crosses all three forks of the Yuba River before reaching Downieville, 43 miles away. Several little towns along the road date back to the Gold Rush.

Despite its Spanish name, North San Juan was as Yankee a town as any in the Northern Mines. It is believed to have been named San Juan by a veteran of the Mexican War who saw a resemblance to a hill in Mexico on which a prison of that name stood. "North" was tacked on when the town acquired a post office in 1857. When San Juan Ridge's hydraulic diggings were being worked, the town was a center for thousands, and it is still the trading center for the few hundred who remain in the area.

Camptonville was named for pioneer blacksmith Robert Campton. The town twice survived the attack of hydraulic monitors by moving each time before its foundations were washed away. Gold was found here in 1852, but real prosperity came only after hydraulic mining started in the late 1860s. By 1866, Camptonville numbered 1,500 residents. A mile-long plank road, the town's main street, was lined on both sides with more than 30 stores, numerous hotels and boarding houses, and many saloons.

Two monuments stand side by side on the west end of town. One is erected to the memory of Lester Pelton, inventor of the Pelton wheel that was so important in the development of hydroelectric power equipment. The other was dedicated by E Clampus Vitus to William "Bull" Meek, who, as the marker reads, was "Stage Driver, Wells Fargo Agent, Teamster, and Merchant."

Meek is believed to be the only regular stage driver in the Northern Mines never to have been robbed by holdup men. Some claimed that he escaped this experience because he regularly carried supplies to a Downieville bordello. According to the theory, the Madam and her ladies used their influence on the region's badmen to keep their supply channel safe.

Goodyear's Bar, at the juncture of Goodyear's Creek and the North Fork of the Yuba River, was named for brothers Andres and Miles Goodyear. The brothers settled at this crossing in 1852, after word got around that $2,000 was taken from a single wheelbarrow load of dirt. But the good times were short lived, and decline was further hastened by a devastating fire that swept through the town in 1864. There is little left today except for a few frame buildings and a sparse population.

Downieville

Downieville is in one of the highest and most rugged regions of the state. The town nestles in a natural wooded amphitheater surrounded by lofty, pine-clad mountains. Though the population (around 400) has dwindled considerably since the days of the Gold Rush, and fire and flood have done their best to destroy this mountain settlement, Downieville is still one of the region's most true-to-life gold towns.

Grizzled stone, brick, and clapboard buildings face on quiet, crooked streets that once echoed with the clatter and rumble of freighters. It's easy to imagine the din that hundreds, sometimes thousands, of miners could raise when they came to town for relaxation and a cup to quench their thirst. Tin-roofed structures from the same period cling to the valley walls above the river, adding to the town's photogenic appeal.

Pick up a copy of the state's oldest continuously published weekly (since 1853), Mountain Messenger, to read while you eat a sandwich at Downieville Bakery. Along Main Street, the iron-shuttered Craycroft Building and the Costa store are tucked in among antique shops and restaurants. On the south side of the Yuba River, all structures date from the 1850s and 1860s. There you'll find a Masonic building, a Native Daughters Hall across the street, a Catholic church, and a Methodist church.

A few blocks east of the museum, the site of Downie's original cabin is marked. The old gallows by the courthouse were used only once, in 1885, to hang one James O'Neal. Little seems to be known about his crime.

First called The Forks, Downieville was renamed for Major William Downie, who wintered here in 1849. After building cabins in anticipation of being snowed in, Downie's party began prospecting to occupy their time. They were pleasantly surprised to find the region rich in gold. By the end of spring, the camp was growing rapidly as news of the rich strikes spread. By June, 1851, about 5,000 people were established here.

Those early argonauts really earned their gold. They worked long hours in icy water, had meager supplies, and had trouble finding any lodging. The trail into Downieville was almost impassable for many months, and commodities were scarce and expensive. Shirts sold for $50, boots were $25 to $150 a pair, and potatoes cost $3 a pound. Supplies improved as the trail got better, but it was a long time before the saloons that boasted many other elegant fixtures had mirrors.

Like many other camps along the forks of the Yuba River, Downieville has contributed its share of true stories of rich strikes. In this case, it's tales like the one of three miners from Tin Cup Diggings who had little trouble filling a cup with dust each day. Others told of a 60-square-foot claim that gave up over $12,000 in 11 days, and a 25-pound nugget of solid gold that was discovered just two miles above the camp.

Another story, often told, strikes a humorous vein. It seems that in 1850 a rascal was caught with a pair of stolen boots. The miners quickly gathered to hold court in the offices of the justice of the peace—a saloon. The culprit's guilt was established, but instead of a flogging or worse, he was ordered to buy the house drinks. After several rounds, the guilty one went unnoticed as he quietly slipped out the door taking with him Exhibit A, the boots, and leaving behind the bill for the drinks.

Historic Attractions

Sierra County Museum

Main Street
Downieville
916/289-3423

The museum building itself is as much a part of the past as the displays it contains. Built in 1852, it once housed a Chinese store and a gambling den. Among the exhibits are a collection of snowshoes for horses and a working model of a stamp mill. *Open daily from Memorial Day through mid-October. Guided tours at 10 A.M. and 4 P.M. Donations requested.*

Gold Exhibit

Sierra County Courthouse
Downieville

The gold nugget replicas you see here are not relics from Gold Rush days (they were mined in the 1930s), but they did come from the Ruby Mine, one of the richest mines around town.

Diversion

Goldpanning

Goldpanning is allowed in downtown Downieville near the fork of the Yuba and Downie rivers. A trail from the heritage park downstream leads to the public panning area (bring your own pan). Panning is also permitted any place along these rivers in the Tahoe National Forest.

Lodging

Sierra Shangri-La

P.O. Box 285
Downieville, CA 95936
916/289-3455   **$$**

On an elbow of the Yuba River two miles east of town sits a cozy lodge with three bedrooms and baths and eight cottages. Cottages have kitchenettes, wood-burning stoves, and decks or patios overlooking the river. Bring charcoal for the barbecue and bathing suits for use in some of the enticing swimming holes. *Open April through December, weather permitting. Reserve well in advance.*

Kenton Mine Lodge

P.O. Box 942
Alleghany, CA 95910
916/287-3212   **$$**

Simplicity and solitude await guests at this rustic hideaway in Kanaka Creek Canyon. There's also gold panning, swimming, and fishing below Alleghany. As they say, part of the fun is getting there: from Highway 49, take the Ridge Road to Alleghany and turn right on Tyler Foote Crossing Road; the last three miles are gravel. The lodge was a boarding house for miners at the century-old Kenton Mine until it and most other area mines shut down in 1939. (The neighboring Oriental Mine was an exception; it operated until 1970.)

Rates for the nine-room lodge and five cabins include breakfast and family-style dinner in the cook house, or you can bring your own food. Children must be supervised carefully as there are a number of abandoned mine shafts around the property.

JUANITA—INNOCENT OR GUILTY?

Downieville wasn't always as quaint and quiet as it is today. In fact, it has the dubious distinction of being the only mining camp in the Gold Rush Country to have hanged a woman.

Everyone seems to agree that Juanita, a fiery Mexican dance hall girl, plunged a knife into the breast of a Scottish miner named Jack Cannon, who had kicked in her door in a drunken rage the night before. But had he come to apologize that morning, or was he still upset?

The story is clouded, and even early newspaper accounts took violently opposing views of the hanging, but most historians believe that Juanita acted in self-defense and was wrongfully lynched. At the time, however, other miners claimed that the stabbing was unprovoked and that Juanita got what she deserved when they hung her.

No one will ever know whether she was actually pregnant as she claimed before they strung her up, or whether this would have made any difference to the mob. Right or wrong, the account electrified California and made news around the world.

A marker in Lion's Memorial Park points out a spot where Juanita allegedly was hung from the bridge.

Dining

Cirino's at The Forks

Main Street
Downieille
916/289-3479 $

You might expect a barbecue since this venerable dining room is decorated with a Western motif, but you'll be surprised by generous family-style Italian dishes redolent with garlic and tangy sauces. Lunch is served on the riverside patio when the weather cooperates. *Open daily for lunch and dinner from the last weekend in April through December. Full bar.*

Side Road

To Forest and Alleghany

You can reach these two old mining camps by taking Mountain House Road south from Goodyear's Bar. Residents are somewhat reclusive and do not look favorably on trespassers, so don't stray onto private property. The road is closed by snow in winter.

The once-lively camp of Forest has undergone many name changes. One authority states it was first called Brownsville after a group of sailors (one named Brown) found gold here in 1852. Later the name was changed to Yomana, an Indian word describing the high bluff above town that was considered to be sacred ground. Another source states it received its present name from a Mrs. Forest Mooney, a woman with a bent for newspaper writing. Evidently her given name inspired her to sign all of her journalistic efforts "Forest City." Historians do agree the last part of the name was dropped in 1895.

The town flourished until the 1880s through profitable drift mining operations, among them the Live Yankee and Bald Mountain mines. When quartz mines were developed on the Alleghany side of Pliocene Ridge, most of Forest's population followed the new strikes.

Forest is now a quiet little hamlet with a handful of residents. A few old buildings (most privately owned) still survive, including a tobacco shop. A weathered Catholic church crowns the hill above, and steep-roofed houses cling to the mountains on either side of the canyon.

Though a fire destroyed much of the center of Alleghany in 1987, you can still see how its homes were built on a bias. Balanced on side hill terraces, they look as if they might fall into the ravine at any minute. At the bottom of the ravine is Kanaka Creek, which was named after Hawaiian prospectors who made the first big strike here in May of 1850. (The word "kanaka" means "men or people" in Hawaiian.)

The most famous of Alleghany's mines was the Original Sixteen to One, named for one of William Jennings Bryan's presidential campaign slogans. Opened in 1896, it provided the economic backbone of the community until its closure in 1965. More than $26 million in gold came from this mine with its unusually rich high-grade ore, and it is acknowledged by the mining fraternity to be one of the richest, and certainly the most spectacular, of California's gold mines.

Recently, a group of miners rediscovered the rich gold-bearing vein in the depths of the mine. According to reports, they are extracting gold worth about one million dollars every week.

Sierra City

Following the old stage road from Downieville, Highway 49 sweeps up the canyon of the North Fork of the Yuba River, past green alpine meadows and apple orchards. You'll see an occasional miner's cabin or farmhouse before you reach Sierra City, where the towering Sierra Buttes overshadow the mountain town.

The Sierra Buttes Mine, riddled with tunnels all the way down to the river, was discovered in 1850 and produced some $17 million in gold. In 1852, the mountains had their revenge when an avalanche of ice and snow crushed every shack and tent in the boom town. It wasn't until 1858 that a permanent settlement was once again established on the townsite. Other catastrophic snow avalanches occurred in 1888 and 1889, killing many people.

Most of the old structures left in town date from the 1870s; the largest is the Busch Building which was built in 1871. Wells Fargo was one of the early tenants. The three-story, tin-roofed Zerloff Hotel was built in the 1860s and is still owned by the same family. The hotel's saloon was one of 22 that operated in Sierra City in the old days.

Historic Attractions

Sierra County Historical Park and Museum at Kentucky Mine

One mile north of town on Highway 49
Sierra City
916/862-1310

A "don't miss" stop at the six-story Kentucky Mine (operated from the 1850s to 1953) allows visitors a good look at one of the few still-operable 10-stamp mills, where ore-breaking rocks were pulverized and gold sifted out. A restored blacksmith shop and miner's cabin also stand on the grounds. The charming museum, which is filled with artifacts donated by local families (including Chinese and Native American art), gives a good sense of early-day Sierra County history. *The park and museum are open 10 A.M. to 5 P.M. Wednesday through Sunday from Memorial Day through September, weekends only through October (weather permitting). Museum admission $1. Guided tours (including museum) are $4 for adults, $2 for children 13-16; younger children are free. Picnic sites. Outdoor summer concerts take place Friday evening during the summer.*

Plumas-Eureka State Park

310 Johnsville Road
Blairsden, CA
916/836-2380

The best preserved wood-constructed town in the Northern Mines, Johnsville lies right in the middle of the park. As a mining camp, Johnsville was a latecomer, built in the 1870s by a company of London investors who bought up land in the vicinity.

Several old buildings (most privately owned) in various stages of collapse make the spot extremely photogenic. A boarding house from mining days has been transformed into a combination park headquarters and museum. Scattered around the grounds are a good collection of old mining implements and wagons. The imposing Plumas-Eureka Mine stamp mill is slowly being restored.

The 50-mile round-trip drive from Sierra City is particularly appealing in autumn when the aspens turn gold. To reach the park, take Highway 49 east a few miles to Bassetts, an important stage stop in the late 1800s, and turn up Gold Lakes Road. When the road is closed in winter, approach the park via Highway 89. *Visitor center and museum open daily from 8 A.M. to 4:30 P.M. in summer; shorter hours the rest of the year. Activities include camping, hiking, and fishing.*

Plumas-Eureka State Park　　　Photo courtesy of Martin Litton

Sierra Valley Museum

City Park
Loyalton, CA
916/993-6750

Browse through this small museum for a look at this valley farming community's past. *Open Wednesday through Saturday afternoons. Donations welcome.*

Lodging

Busch & Heringlake Country Inn

P.O. Box 68
Sierra City, CA 96125
916/862-1501 **$$**

Formerly an 1871 Wells Fargo Express stop, this surprisingly sophisticated two-story inn has four upstairs rooms, all with private baths (two have Jacuzzi tubs) and a nice dining room on the lower floor.

Herrington's Sierra Pines Resort

P.O. Box 235
Sierra City, CA 96125
916/862-1151 **$-$$**

Most of the 20 motel-type units have views of the river from their covered decks. The restaurant (see below) is not only convenient but one of the area's best, especially if you like fresh trout. *Open April to December (weather permitting).*

Sierra Buttes Inn

Sierra City, CA 96125
916/862-1300 **$**

Though most people come for the food (see below), this century-old inn has 11 rooms for rent, six with private bath.

High Country Inn

Highway 49 and Gold Lake Road s
east of Sierra City
HCR 2, Box 7
Sierra City, CA 96125
916/862-1501 **$$**

For grand views of the Sierra Buttes, step onto the deck of this inviting four-room lodge. When the weather turns cool, you can curl up on a couch beside the fireplace. Rooms are spacious; the Sierra Buttes Suite has a fireplace and a huge bathroom complete with flannel nightshirts and terry robes. A wholesome complimentary breakfast is included in the rate.

Dining

Herrington's Sierra Pines Resort

Sierra City
916/862-1151 **$**

This riverside restaurant specializes in trout fresh from their own pond. Also on the menu are steak, shrimp, and home-baked breads and desserts. Sunday breakfast offerings include strawberry pancakes, Eggs Benedict, biscuits and gravy, and more. *Breakfast, lunch, and dinner daily May to November. Full bar.*

Sierra Buttes Inn

Sierra City
916/862-1300 **$**

The wonderful western-style bar has country music on the jukebox and mounted animal heads on the walls. The dining room serves food just as "down home" and delicious—chicken-fried steak, prime rib, and teriyaki chicken. *Open for dinner daily in summer, Thusrsday through Sunday in winter.*

The Iron Door

Plumas Eureka State Park
Johnsville
916/836-2376 **$**

Campers can dine out at this park-operated restaurant. The venerable dining room occupies the former site of a century-old general store and post office building. The menu features beef, lobster, and fowl. *Dinner daily from April to October. Full bar.*

Side Road

East on Highway 49

East of Sierra City, Highway 49 continues its climb up the canyon of the North Fork of the Yuba River to the 6,701-foot summit of Yuba Pass, and then drops down quickly to the floor of a broad valley. Travelers find overnight accommodations and a few places to eat in the farming center of Loyalton. Or, plan a picnic in the city park before you wander through the small Sierra Valley Museum.

A few miles farther east, the Mother Lode Highway ends abruptly in the tiny town of Vinton.

Photo courtesy of the Golden Chain Council

The Sierra Buttes tower above the Yuba River Canyon and can be seen from many spots in the Sacramento Valley.

Oroville

Though Oroville is not on Highway 49, it has a Gold Rush past. Miners came to the area in 1849, and it has been the scene of all types of mining from placer to hydraulic. Gold-dredging started here and spread throughout the world. The ancient river bed on which Oroville is built is so rich in gold that a dredging company once offered to move the whole town just for the right to mine the ground on which it stood. Thousands of acres of waste tailings were used in the construction of the Oroville Dam.

Historic Attractions

Chinese Temple

1500 Broderick Street
Oroville, CA
916/538-2496

This 1863 temple is now the sole survivor of a Chinatown that was once among the largest in the West. Tours of several temples and courtyards reveal a wealth of arts and artifacts, including a hall of magnificent tapestries donated by descendants of the original Chinese community. *Open daily except Monday from February through mid-December for self-guiding tours; hours vary. Admission $2 adults; children under 12 free.*

Lott Home

Montgomery Street between 3rd and 4th avenues
Oroville, CA
916/538-2497

Another worthwhile stop is at the Judge C. F. Lott House in Sank Park. The two-story frame residence has been carefully restored to its 1856 grandeur and now serves as a museum for period furnishings and displays of historic photographs. *Open Sunday through Tuesday and Friday afternoons. Free admission. Picnic facilities in the park.*

Diversions

Lake Oroville Visitor Center

Lake Oroville
916/538-2219

This center overlooks Lake Oroville, one of Northern California's major recreational areas, and Oroville Dam. The center displays dioramas of the Gold Rush era, state water projects, wildlife, and local Maidu Indians. Films are shown on request. *Open daily. Free admission.*

Lodging

Grand Manor Inn

1470 Feather River Boulevard
Oroville, CA 95965
916/533-9673 $

This Best Western motel has 54 attractive rooms, all with refrigerators and cable television. Travelers make good use of the pool and coin-operated laundry.

Dining

The Depot

2191 High Street
Oroville
916/534-9101 $

With one of Oroville's best salad bars, this casual restaurant is popular with residents. *Open daily for lunch and dinner (dinner only Sunday). Full bar.*

Side Roads

North of Oroville

Scores of mining camps were once located in the hill region north of Oroville. Today, most are marked only by unkempt cemeteries. The almost-ghost town of Cherokee (population 10 to 12) is an exception. From the few weather-beaten buildings that remain, it's hard to imagine that this was a thriving town in 1870. But 7,000 people lived here, and the town boasted three churches, eight hotels, three schools, and 17 saloons. Also that year, some five million dollars in gold was taken from the nearby hills by giant hydraulic nozzles.

The first diamonds ever discovered in the United States were picked out of a Cherokee sluice box in 1866. There are many stories about miners finding big gems, and even a far-fetched tale about a fortunate woman who found a two-carat stone in the craw of a Christmas turkey that allegedly had spent its youth in Cherokee.

The ruins of Cherokee's Spring Valley Assay Office and an old boarding house have been converted into a museum (open 11 A.M. to 3 P.M. on weekends). Another ramshackle one-room building is crammed with memorabilia of a visit from President Rutherford B. Hayes in 1890. Pioneers slumber eternally in the iron-gated cemetery.

To reach the town from Oroville, follow Cherokee Road 10 miles north. Another former mining camp, Oregon City, lies about half-way between Oroville and Cherokee, on a side road. Today, all that is left of the camp are an old schoolhouse and a cemetery.

Forbestown Road

If you roam around the countryside east of Oroville, you'll find some remnants of mining days. Forbestown Road leads to a once-profitable mining camp founded in 1850 by pioneer B. F. Forbes. The town was an active part of the gold mining scene for about 50 years, but all that remains of that era is the Masonic Hall, which was built in 1855. The original townsite was about a mile north of the present post office and stores.

La Porte Road

The La Porte Road heads east through mountainous terrain, passing by former mining camps like Strawberry Valley, La Porte, Gibsonville, and Howland Flat. It ends at State Highway 70 near the town of Quincy.

In the 1850s, Strawberry Valley's streets were lined with dozens of stores and hotels. At that time, when the little community was a trading center for the surrounding mines. The venerable Columbus Hotel is the solitary reminder of those lively days. There is some confusion about the origins of the town's name: either it came from wild berries that grew in the area, or it is the combination of the names of two miners, Straw and Berry.

La Porte, originally called Rabbit Creek, was a well-populated hydraulic mining center before the Anti-Debris Act stopped that form of mining. Today it's only a shadow of itself. The crumbling walls of the Wells Fargo building and the Union Hotel serve as reminders of the past. Lotta Crabtree, the most famous of the Gold Rush Country's entertainers, lived here as a child, but her home was destroyed by fire. A plaque at the west end of town marks the site of the Rabbit Creek Hotel, and commemorates the discovery of gold on Rabbit Creek in 1850.

Gibsonville is perched on a windswept ridge overlooking Slate Creek. The town's few remaining houses have been bleached almost white by the weather. Its name honors the prospector who made the original gold strike along the creek. Gibson also made another rich strike, but refused to divulge its location to his comrades. The resulting hostility caused the group to scatter, and resulted in new discoveries in all directions. The strike at nearby Howland Flat made that camp one of the region's most populous for a short time. Poker Flat, three miles from Howland Flat, was the setting for one of Bret Harte's most famous stories, *The Outcasts of Poker Flat.*

Other picturesquely-named mining camps around the area were established about the same time. Nothing remains to distinguish Queen City, Poverty Hill, or Scales. Port Wine, however, is still marked by a stone building, a cemetery, and a large pile of tailings. The camp was named by prospectors who found a cask of wine hidden in a canyon.

TRYING YOUR LUCK WITH A GOLD PAN

One good way to catch some of the spirit of the colorful Gold Rush days is to try your luck with a gold pan. Children especially will find a short session with a pan exciting. Several Gold Country operators offer panning opportunities, from an hour's indoctrination to all-day trips. If you choose to pan on your own, make sure you are on public land, such as a national forest. Plan your trip for spring and early summer; small streams may be dry by midsummer.

Gold panner's gear

The simple penknife was the earliest tool used by argonauts to extract gold from streams. By probing rocks in the stream with a knife, they might bring up hunks of the precious metal with one stab. Today, panning tools are not hard to come by. Those you don't have around the house, you can find at hardware stores and lapidary shops in the Gold Country.

Basic requirements: gold pan (10 to 18 inches in diameter), pointed shovel for working gravel, prospector's pick, long-handled spoon or butcher knife for digging into crevices, bucket for gravel and concentrate, tweezers for handling tiny grains, hand lens for tweezer-sized grains; magnet to remove black (magnetic) sand from concentrate, and a small bottle with a stopper for water in which to store gold flakes.

How to pan

Gold panning is a sifting process in which water is used to float off lighter material, allowing heavy gold-bearing particles to settle.

Fill your pan with bedrock material and submerge it in water. Pick out large gravel pieces, washing them with your fingers until silt is removed. Then raise the pan so that the material is just below the surface. Tipping the pan slightly away from you, move it in a horizontal circle with a slight jerk each time around, swirling the water and allowing the light sand and coarse gravel to fall gently over the lip of the pan.

Bringing the pan out of the water, tilt it away from you. Alternately dip and rotate the pan out of the water, letting the water carry away the lighter gravels. Use the back of your hand to brush them out. Continue this until only the finest sand remains in the pan.

Then put the concentrate in a bucket to be panned out at the end of the day in a "clean-up pan." At this time, after carefully removing any excess sand, a magnet can be used to remove the last of the black sand.

How to size up a placer

Without going into the geology of placer mining, you can learn a few things a miner looks for before he begins to work the gravels of a particular stream. Coarse gold tends to be deposited near the point where it enters the stream. A beginner will probably have more luck in locations where a stream descends gradually, at least one-half to two feet per 100 feet.

A stream will deposit gold-rich gravels wherever the current slows, where the stream grade decreases, and where the river widens, deepens, turns, or joins another stream. Likely panning sites are at the upstream end of gravel bars and on the lee side of boulders and obstructions.

Since gold tends to settle at the very bottom of coarse material, a shallow gravel bar will be easier to work than a deep one. Look for bedrock ledges or riffles in the water or on the immediate banks. Gold often settles in small pockets of gravels in bedrock. Many prospectors use a long-handled spoon or knife to get into crevices, as they know that any soft material extracted is probably worth panning.

You find gold where other heavy materials collect. This means that streaks of black and colored sands are promising. One heavy material that may indicate the presence of gold is fools' gold (pyrite). Unlike gold, pyrite is often found in cubes, has a brassy luster on freshly broken surfaces, and will fracture rather than crush as gold will. Gold has a yellow color all its own. It has a luster in sun or shade, cuts easily with a knife, and never scales or fractures.

Mica, too, glitters in a stream and is often mistaken for gold. Mica is light, settles slowly in the water (in contrast to the way gold drops), and scales into flakes.

GLOSSARY
OF MINING TERMS

Argonaut—term used interchangeably with "49er" to refer to the first goldseekers in California.

Assay office—a place that evaluated mineral content of ore by chemical analysis.

Bar—pertaining to banks of sand or gravel that extended into a river. Later used to describe any camp that sprang up alongside a river bar, such as Chili Bar.

Bullion—unminted gold or silver. Usually melted into bricks or bars for easy storage.

Claim—piece of land that was located, or "staked out," by a miner for working. Miners soon realized they needed a system for filing claims. They drew up regulations specifying the size of claims, and decided how disputes would be adjudicated. These early agreements were the basis for mining laws all over the West.

Color—term usually used to indicate finding evidence of gold.

Diggings—early mining term referring to a claim that was being worked for gold.

Dry diggings—a mining claim worked for gold in a region where water has to be brought in to work the gravels.

Dust—minute particles of gold taken by placer mining and used as a form of money. In many camps, $1 was the amount of "dust" that could be held between thumb and forefinger; also called "pinch."

Fandango hall—a Mexican drinking and gambling spot. Named after the "fandango," a castanet-clacking dance.

Flume—inclined trough, usually built of wood, used to convey water for long distances.

Glory hole—hole from which an unusually rich deposit of gold-bearing ore was extracted.

Going to see the elephant—phrase used by greenhorns to describe their anticipated experiences in the gold fields.

Gulch—deep, narrow valley or ravine. Because of their location, many mining camps contained the word "gulch" as part of their name.

Hardrock (quartz) mining—the underground method of mining accomplished by sinking a shaft deep into ground containing a vein or ore pocket, with drifts (tunnels) radiating out on various levels.

Headframe—also known as "gallows frame." Wooden structure erected over the top of a shaft and used in raising and lowering ore buckets.

Highgrade—gold-rich ore. A "highgrader" was someone who removed gold from a claim illegally.

Hydraulicking—an effective but destructive method of mining. Water under pressure was directed at soft gravels, causing dirt to run down into sluice boxes and banks to disintegrate.

I.O.O.F.—a fraternal order to which large numbers of gold miners belonged. Also known as Odd Fellows.

Joss house—Chinese temple used as a place of worship. An excellent example is in Oroville.

Lode—an underground gold-bearing vein.

Monitor—huge nozzle used to direct jets of water in hydraulic mining. Sometimes referred to as "giant."

Nugget—lump of gold of any size, usually larger than the head of a match. The largest nugget found weighed 195 pounds.

Panning—a simple, but slow, method of mining. Gravels from the stream bed are washed in a pan, causing lighter materials to spill over the side and heavier gold-bearing particles to settle to the bottom.

Pay dirt—expression describing gold-rich ore taken from claims.

Pelton wheel—a huge turbine waterwheel that produced the power to run mining equipment. The wheel was invented by Lester Pelton in 1878. Examples can be seen today at the North Star Mining Museum in Grass Valley and at Sierra County Historical Park and Museum near Sierra City.

Placer mining—a process of extracting surface gold from ore-bearing gravels by panning, dredging, and sluicing. This was the method used by California's first prospectors. Because water was essential to the process, most placer claims were located along creeks, streams, and rivers.

Pocket—a small concentration of gold-bearing gravel.

Poke—amount of gold dust or nuggets a miner owned; usually carried in a crude leather pouch.

Quartz—mineral generally found in large masses or veins. The quartz in the Sierra Nevada was mined for its gold content.

Retort—furnace used to heat gold and mercury. Mercury was vaporized and the gold remaining was formed into bars.

Rocker—rectangular wooden box set on rockers, used in mining. The rocking motion caused the mixture of dirt and water to flow through the box, with gold-bearing particles trapped by riffles.

Sluice box—a modified rocker. Water power forced dirt through the box, with gold-bearing particles caught by riffles.

Stamp mill—a mill built to break up and grind gold-bearing ore. A mill could have any number of "stamps," which were the metal arms that raised and lowered to crush the ore so that the gold could be extracted. A "10-stamp" mill was twice as large as a "5-stamp" mill, for example.

Strike—a new-found concentration of gold rich enough to be mined profitably.

Tailings—waste material left after gold-bearing ore was processed.

Vein—route followed by gold from the lower depths of the earth toward the surface.

Worked out—referring to an area from which all gold was thought to have been extracted.

THE TIME OF THE ARGONAUTS
An Historical Chronology

It is often difficult to keep the complete picture of the California Gold Rush in mind as you travel along Highway 49. Each town offers but a small bit of history, and the grand scheme of things tends to get lost in a morass of dates, names, and details. This brief chronology is intended as a general reference guide to the major events of the time.

Because of space limitations, some events have been omitted, but enough is included to give you a general idea of how the Gold Rush spread throughout California. Emphasis is placed on the years 1848 to 1851, since this was the the primary period of discovery.

Notable political events are also included to keep the Gold Rush in proper perspective with the development of California as a territory and state. Additional details are readily available in any of the well-written histories of the state. Of particular interest are *Historic Spots in California* by Mildred Brooke Hoover, Hero Eugene Rensch, and Ethel Grace Rensch (Stanford University Press, Stanford, CA, 94305), *California Place Names* by Erwin G. Gudde (University of California Press, Berkeley, CA, 94704), and *Gold Rush Country* by Truman, Watkins, and Olmsted (California Historical Society, San Francisco, CA, 94103).

1839 August. Swiss-born John Sutter arrives at the confluence of the Sacramento and American rivers to start Northern California's first inland settlement.

1841 November 4. The first California pioneers, organized by John Bidwell, arrive in the San Joaquin Valley after leaving Independence, Missouri, on May 19.

1842 March. While digging onions, rancher Francisco Lopez finds gold in the San Fernando Hills, about 45 miles north of Los Angeles. Within two months, about 100 miners are working the placers. But the gold supply is limited and when John Bidwell visits the site in 1845, he finds about 30 miners working hard for 30 cents a day.

1845 July. James Marshall arrives at Sutter's Fort on a wagon train from Oregon.

1846 March. Supposedly acting on orders from President Polk, Captain John C. Fremont raises the American flag on a peak in the Salinas Valley. The gesture is ineffective, and Mexican rule continues in Alta, California.

1846 May 13. War begins between the U.S. and Mexico.

1846 June 14. Believing that the *Californios* (Mexican settlers) are going to run them out of the state, a group of Yankee ranchers ride into Sonoma, capture General Mariano Vallejo, and declare California the Bear Flag Republic.

1846 July 7. Commodore John Sloat lands the U.S. Pacific Fleet at Monterey, raises the American flag, and proclaims California part of the United States. Two days later, the U.S. flag replaces the Bear Flag at Sonoma, and a flag is raised on Yerba Buena Island in the San Francisco Bay.

1846 October. The first storms of what will be an exceptionally heavy winter trap the immigrant wagon train led by George Donner in the Sierra. By spring, 39 of the 87 members of the train will be dead of cold and starvation in the greatest tragedy of the California migration.

1847 January 13. The war in California ends when Captain Fremont and General Pico, leader of the *Californios*, sign the Cahuenga Capitulation.

1847 Late January. The Mormon Battalion (300 recruits from Utah) arrive to fight in the war with Mexico. They are too late for the fighting, but some decide to stay and work for John Sutter.

1847 February 10. John Fremont becomes the owner of a big tract of land near Mariposa which appears worthless at the time, but ultimately will become the richest of the Southern Mines.

1847 May 16. At Sutter's instruction, James Marshall sets out for the foothills to select a site for a sawmill. Marshall selects a valley on the American River that Native Americans call *Culluma*.

1847 August 27. Sutter and Marshall sign an agreement to build the mill, with Sutter to provide the manpower (primarily members of the Mormon Battalion) and Marshall the know-how. Work begins in September.

1848 January 24. While examining the tailrace of the partially completed mill, Marshall notices something glittering in the rocks. He picks up a small piece of metal, and after a few preliminary tests decides that what he has found is gold.

1848 January 28. Marshall arrives at Sutter's Fort with his precious metal. Sutter subjects it to several more tests and proves conclusively that Marshall has discovered gold.

1848 February 2. The treaty of Guadalupe Hidalgo is signed, formally ending the Mexican War. The California territory is formally ceded to the United States.

1848 February 6. Though pledged to secrecy about Marshall's discovery, the workers at the mill become the first argonauts by sneaking off to pry gold nuggets out of the rock with penknives.

1848 Mid-February. Sutter sends Charles Bennett on a secret mission to Monterey to secure land rights at Coloma. But Bennett cannot keep the discovery of gold a secret and spreads the word to everyone he meets.

1848 March. Mormon Island becomes the first mining camp outside of Coloma. Sutter reports that he is losing all of his men to the gold fields.

1848 March 11. The sawmill at Coloma is finished. It will be operated sporadically for about five years before being torn down by miners who had denuded the surrounding area of trees and needed the mill's lumber to build cabins.

1848 March 15. The first story of the gold discovery is printed in a San Francisco newspaper, but not many people pay any attention to the report.

1848 Late March. John Bidwell visits Coloma and decides there must be gold in the northern mountains. He makes a big strike at Bidwell's Bar in April.

1848 April 1. San Francisco sends a special messenger to the East Coast with news of the rumored gold discovery.

1848 May. By now, 800 miners are working at Coloma, Mormon Island, Kelsey's Diggings, and other areas on both sides of Sutter's Mill. One of the richest strikes of all is made at Dry Diggins (ultimately to become Placerville) and gold is discovered on the Yuba River near Long Barn. Claude Chana and a group of miners make a strike at North Fork Dry Diggins (later to become Auburn). George Angel builds a trading Post on Calaveritas Creek and Angels Camp is born. Drytown is settled. After early skepticism, San Franciscans are finally convinced that gold really has been found, and the rush to the foothills begins.

1848 June 1. The number of miners now working the foothills is estimated at 2,000.

1848 June 14. Almost everyone in San Franisco departs for the gold fields. The last of the San Francisco newspapers suspends operation for lack of readers; practically all other business in the city has also been suspended.

1848 June 20. A special messenger arrives in Monterey with a pocketful of nuggets dug near Coloma. Residents, finally convinced of Marshall's discovery, make a mass exodus.

1848 June 24. A newspaper in Hawaii reports the discovery, and the first ships loaded with argonauts leave the islands in July.

1848 July. Some 4,000 miners are now working in the foothills. Col. R. B. Mason, Military Governor of California, visits Coloma and confirms the richness of the diggings. News of the discovery reaches Los Angeles and the first miners start north. John Sutter and a crew of Native Americans find gold at Sutter Creek, and John and Daniel Murphy start the town that is to carry their name.

1848 August. First rumors reach the East Coast, but there is no official confirmation yet. A Chilean ship reaches Valparaiso with the news, and several thousand men start immediately for California. When ships from Hawaii stop in Oregon en route to San Francisco, the news of gold is spread, and wagon trains start south. New mining camps spring up at Jackson, Woods Crossing, Tuttletown, Fiddletown, and Timbuctoo. Friendly Native Americans lead James Carson to gold on Carson Creek. Sonorian Camp (Sonora) becomes the southernmost mining camp to be settled in 1848.

1848 September. Heat and sickness in the mines cause the weakest men to abandon the diggings and return to the valleys; many settle around Sutter's Fort. Also, Washington D.C. receives official confirmation of Marshall's discovery on this date.

1848 October. The number of miners has grown to 8,000. Mexico learns of the discovery, and a great migration is prepared for the following spring.

1848 November. Mokelumne Hill is founded. With the advent of winter, many miners are forced out of the hill; only the hardy continue working through the winter. On the East Coast, the first ships loaded with would-be miners leave for California; more get ready to sail from New York, Boston, Salem, Norfolk, Philadelphia, and Baltimore.

1848 December 5. President Polk's message to Congress confirms the California gold discovery. His message is backed up by a box filled with gold dust that is placed on public display. Gold fever takes hold. When a flood of miners reach Coloma, James Marshall and John Sutter sell most of their interests.

1848 December 23. A newspaper in Sydney, Australia, publishes news of the discovery; hundreds of miners set sail.

1849 January. Five California trading and mining companies are started in London, and all of Europe begins to send ships loaded with miners.

1849 February 28. The *California*, first of the Pacific Mail Line steamships, arrives in San Francisco with the first load of 49ers.

1849 Spring. With the advent of spring, prospecting resumes. Gold is discovered in Jacksonville, mining begins at Jenny Lind, and Goodyear's Bar is settled by Miles Goodyear.

1849 May. The great procession of overland wagon trains begins from St. Joseph and Independence, Missouri. In Sonora, Mexico, some 4,000 miners start their way north.

1849 July. The first of the overland wagon trains arrives in the Sacramento Valley. By now, 600 vessels have arrived in San Francisco Bay, and both crews and passengers head immediately for the mines.

1849 September. The first miners work the gravels at Downieville; the town is started in November by Major Downie.

1849 October. The first of the European emigrants begin to arrive. Dr. A. B. Caldwell builds a general store on Deer Creek and Nevada City is born. Chinese Camp is settled. James Savage begins mining at Big Oak Flat, and the first miners set up camp at Coulterville, French Corral, Volcano, San Andreas, Groveland, Shaws Flat, and Oroville.

1849 November 13. A state constitution is ratified, a governor is elected, and senators and assembly are named—even though the California territory is not legally a state.

1849 Winter. It is estimated that 42,000 argonauts have arrived by land during the year, and another 39,000 have come by sea from all parts of the world. Heavy rains force many miners out of the hills and into Sacramento and San Francisco. Their presence prompts the cities to realize their inadequacies and promotes improvements such as paved streets, sidewalks, and sewers.

1850 Spring. In the Southern Mines, Mount Bullion is settled, and the first private mint in California opens at Mt. Ophir.

1850 March. Mexicans discover gold a few miles north of Sonora. On March 27, a group of American miners also hit pay dirt, and the rush is started at Columbia.

1850 April. Yankee dislike for foreigners results in the legislative adoption of a Foreign Miners Tax of $20 a month, renewable every month. Supposedly leveled against all "furriners," it is enforced chiefly against the Mexicans and the Chinese.

1850 June. An accidental discovery of gold-bearing quartz on Gold Hill starts the rush to Grass Valley.

1850 Summer. Kanaka Creek below Alleghany is first mined by Hawaiians. A new settlement grows at Growlersburg (Georgetown), and mining starts in Onion Valley near La Port. Michigan Bluff and Sierra City have their first success; Washington is founded as Indian Camp.

1850 September 9. California is admitted into the Union as the 31st state.

1850 October 18. The steamer Oregon brings the news of statehood to San Francisco.

1850 Winter. During this year, 55,000 people have arrived on the overland cavarans, and another 36,000 have come by sea.

1851 February. The first quartz mine in Amador County is discovered at Amador Creek. This, plus the findings at Grass Valley, start a big boom in quartz mining.

1851 March 14. The Foreign Miners Tax is repealed, at least temporarily.

1851 April. Gold is discovered in Australia, and the tide of argonauts across the Pacific is reversed. Virtually all of the main California gold fields are settled by now, and prospectors must move on to find new diggings. When gold is discovered in Oregon's Rogue River country, more miners give up California in search of greener pastures.

1852 May 4. A new license fee of $3 (later to be raised to $4) is assessed against all foreign miners.

1852 Summer. Mining starts at La Grange and Camptonville.

1853 March. E. E. Matteson first forces water under pressure through a nozzle to wash a gravel bank, and hydraulic mining begins.

1853 Summer. Lola Montez settles in Grass Valley; Christian Kientz discovers gold at North San Juan. Michael Savage begins mining at Forest Hill. Iowa Hill becomes a boom town. After a time of depression, confidence is restored that quartz mining will last for decades.

1854 Spring. Bret Harte arrives in California for a 17-year stay, most of which is spent far from the mines. But his brief experiences with frontiersmen provide enough material for many literary works.

1854 Summer. Lotta Crabtree gives her performance for the miners at La Porte and is launched on a long and successful stage career.

1854 Autumn. Gold is discovered on the Kern River in Southern California, drawing more miners from the north. Still others sail for Peru, but the stories of rich mines there turn out to be only rumors.

1855 August 11. Tom Bell attempts the first stage robbery for gold, but he is foiled and ultimately captured.

1859 July 1. The *Nevada Journal* in Nevada City publishes the results of assays of ore specimens brought from the state of Nevada, which shows that silver as well as gold has been discovered. The great rush to the Comstock begins. Many historians regard this as the official end of the California Gold Rush.

1860 April 13. The first westbound rider of the Pony Express reaches San Francisco after leaving St. Joseph, Missouri, on April 3.

1861 Summer. Mark Twain arrives in the West. He will stay until 1865 and write some of the best Gold Country stories ever published.

1862 Winter. Unprecedented storms produce terrible floods that badly damage river communities and illustrate how unrestricted hydraulic mining chokes the river beds.

1877 Summer. Black Bart stages his first successful holdup.

1880 June 18. John Sutter dies in Pennsylvania.

1884 January 23. The Sawyer Decision following passage of the Anti-Debris Act of 1883 closes all the hydraulic mines in California.

1885 August 10. James Marshall dies at Kelsey.

1893 Summer. The Caminetti Act permits hydraulic mines to reopen if debris dams are built to catch all of the silt before it can clog the rivers. A few attempts are made to meet the requirements, but the cost is too great and hydraulic mining is abandoned completely.

CALENDAR OF EVENTS

Listed below is a sampling of festivities that take place throughout the year in the Gold Rush Country. Although most celebrations are held annually, some depend on variables such as weather and funds. Phone the indicated numbers to check on definite dates for a specific event, or call the appropriate county Chamber of Commerce for additional information on events occurring in that area.

MARCH

Daffodil Hill bulb show begins in mid-March
Volcano area, (209) 223-0608

Annual Storytelling Festival, Mariposa County Fairgrounds
Mariposa (209) 966-2456

Dandelion Days, flea market held near St. Patrick's Day
Jackson, (209) 223-0350

APRIL

Jazz Festival
Jackson, (209) 223-0350

Wild West Stampede, rodeo and horse show
Auburn, (916) 887-2111

MAY

Western Weekend (music, arts and crafts, rodeo)
Oakhurst, (209) 683-4636

Music at the Wineries (wine, appetizers, and music)
Shenandoah Valley, (209) 267-0211

Springtime in the Pines Quilt Show
Grass Valley, (916) 273-4667

Firemen's Muster, vintage fire fighting displays
Columbia S.H.P., (209) 532-0150

Coarsegold Rodeo
(209) 683-8383

Jumping Frog Jubilee, Calaveras County Fairgrounds
Angels Camp, (209) 736-0049

Snyder's Pow Wow
Valley Springs, (209) 736-0049

Gold Rush Days
Mariposa, (209) 966-3155

Bonanza Gold Show, Mother Lode Fairgrounds
Sonora, (209) 533-4420

Gold 'n Fiddle Festival
Auburn, (916) 888-8682

JUNE

Italian Picnic and Parade, Sutter Hill
Sutter Creek, (209) 223-0350

Amador City Fiesta
(209) 223-0350

Malakoff Diggins Homecoming Celebration
North Bloomfield, (916) 265-4650

Bicycle Classic, Father's Day weekend
Nevada City, (916) 265-2692

JULY

Amador County Fair
Plymouth, (209) 223-0350

Gunfighters' Rendezvous, western shoot-outs
Jamestown, (209) 984-3851

Miners Picnic, Empire Mine S. H. P.
Grass Valley, (916) 273-8522

AUGUST

El Dorado County Fair, Fairgrounds
Placerville, (916) 621-5885

Miners Day Weekend
Downieville, (916) 289-3560

SEPTEMBER

Mountain Peddlers' Flea Market and Craft Fair
Oakhurst, (209) 683-7766

Big Time Indian Days, Indian Grinding Rock S.H.P.
Volcano, (209) 296-7488

Constitution Day, Civil War Re-enactment
Nevada City, (916) 265-2692

Black Bart Days
San Andreas, (209) 736-0040

Apple Hill Harvest, apples, food, and crafts
Camino, (916) 644-3970

OCTOBER

Gem & Mineral Show, Nevada County Fairgrounds
    Grass Valley, (916) 432-9677

NOVEMBER

A Miner's Christmas Carol, Fallon Theater
    Columbia S.H.P., (209) 532-4644

DECEMBER

Annual Cornish Christmas Celebration, weekends
    downtown Grass Valley, (916) 272-8315

Festival of Lights and Scottish Christmas Walk
    Volcano, (209) 223-0350

Victorian Christmas Celebration
    Nevada City, (916) 265-2692

INDEX

About the Author

Barbara Braasch brings an insider's look to *California's Gold Rush Country*. She lives in a century-old, tin-roofed miner's cabin in Sutter Creek, the heart of the Mother Lode, and was the author of *Sunset Magazine & Books'* former guide to the area. An active member of the Society of American Travel Writers, she has written 14 travel guides and contributes articles to *Grolier Encyclopedia Americana, San Jose Mercury News, San Francisco Examiner, Sacramento Magazine, GuestWest, Sasquatch Books,* and *Toyon Hill Press.*